A treatise on regeneration. By Peter Van Mastricht, D.D. Professor of Divinity in the Universities of Francfort, Duisburgh, and Utrecht. Extracted from his system of divinity

Peter van Mastricht

A treatise on regeneration. By Peter Van Mastricht, D.D. Professor of Divinity in the Universities of Francfort, Duisburgh, and Utrecht. Extracted from his system of divinity, called Theologia theoretico-practica; and faithfully translated into English; w

Mastricht, Peter van
ESTCID: W028368
Reproduction from British Library
Half-title: Dr. Van Mastricht, on regeneration. Advertised as "just published" in the Connecticut journal, New Haven, Sept. 7, 1770. Dated 1769 by Evans. "Errata."--p. 94.
New-Haven : Printed and sold by Thomas and Samuel Green, in the Old-Council-Chamber, [1770].
viii,9-94,[2]p. ; 8°

Eighteenth Century
Collections Online
Print Editions

Gale ECCO Print Editions

Relive history with *Eighteenth Century Collections Online*, now available in print for the independent historian and collector. This series includes the most significant English-language and foreign-language works printed in Great Britain during the eighteenth century, and is organized in seven different subject areas including literature and language; medicine, science, and technology; and religion and philosophy. The collection also includes thousands of important works from the Americas.

The eighteenth century has been called "The Age of Enlightenment." It was a period of rapid advance in print culture and publishing, in world exploration, and in the rapid growth of science and technology – all of which had a profound impact on the political and cultural landscape. At the end of the century the American Revolution, French Revolution and Industrial Revolution, perhaps three of the most significant events in modern history, set in motion developments that eventually dominated world political, economic, and social life.

In a groundbreaking effort, Gale initiated a revolution of its own: digitization of epic proportions to preserve these invaluable works in the largest online archive of its kind. Contributions from major world libraries constitute over 175,000 original printed works. Scanned images of the actual pages, rather than transcriptions, recreate the works *as they first appeared.*

Now for the first time, these high-quality digital scans of original works are available via print-on-demand, making them readily accessible to libraries, students, independent scholars, and readers of all ages.

For our initial release we have created seven robust collections to form one the world's most comprehensive catalogs of 18th century works.

Initial Gale ECCO Print Editions collections include:

History and Geography
Rich in titles on English life and social history, this collection spans the world as it was known to eighteenth-century historians and explorers. Titles include a wealth of travel accounts and diaries, histories of nations from throughout the world, and maps and charts of a world that was still being discovered. Students of the War of American Independence will find fascinating accounts from the British side of conflict.

Social Science

Delve into what it was like to live during the eighteenth century by reading the first-hand accounts of everyday people, including city dwellers and farmers, businessmen and bankers, artisans and merchants, artists and their patrons, politicians and their constituents. Original texts make the American, French, and Industrial revolutions vividly contemporary.

Medicine, Science and Technology

Medical theory and practice of the 1700s developed rapidly, as is evidenced by the extensive collection, which includes descriptions of diseases, their conditions, and treatments. Books on science and technology, agriculture, military technology, natural philosophy, even cookbooks, are all contained here.

Literature and Language

Western literary study flows out of eighteenth-century works by Alexander Pope, Daniel Defoe, Henry Fielding, Frances Burney, Denis Diderot, Johann Gottfried Herder, Johann Wolfgang von Goethe, and others. Experience the birth of the modern novel, or compare the development of language using dictionaries and grammar discourses.

Religion and Philosophy

The Age of Enlightenment profoundly enriched religious and philosophical understanding and continues to influence present-day thinking. Works collected here include masterpieces by David Hume, Immanuel Kant, and Jean-Jacques Rousseau, as well as religious sermons and moral debates on the issues of the day, such as the slave trade. The Age of Reason saw conflict between Protestantism and Catholicism transformed into one between faith and logic -- a debate that continues in the twenty-first century.

Law and Reference

This collection reveals the history of English common law and Empire law in a vastly changing world of British expansion. Dominating the legal field is the *Commentaries of the Law of England* by Sir William Blackstone, which first appeared in 1765. Reference works such as almanacs and catalogues continue to educate us by revealing the day-to-day workings of society.

Fine Arts

The eighteenth-century fascination with Greek and Roman antiquity followed the systematic excavation of the ruins at Pompeii and Herculaneum in southern Italy; and after 1750 a neoclassical style dominated all artistic fields. The titles here trace developments in mostly English-language works on painting, sculpture, architecture, music, theater, and other disciplines. Instructional works on musical instruments, catalogs of art objects, comic operas, and more are also included.

The BiblioLife Network

This project was made possible in part by the BiblioLife Network (BLN), a project aimed at addressing some of the huge challenges facing book preservationists around the world. The BLN includes libraries, library networks, archives, subject matter experts, online communities and library service providers. We believe every book ever published should be available as a high-quality print reproduction; printed on-demand anywhere in the world. This insures the ongoing accessibility of the content and helps generate sustainable revenue for the libraries and organizations that work to preserve these important materials.

The following book is in the "public domain" and represents an authentic reproduction of the text as printed by the original publisher. While we have attempted to accurately maintain the integrity of the original work, there are sometimes problems with the original work or the micro-film from which the books were digitized. This can result in minor errors in reproduction. Possible imperfections include missing and blurred pages, poor pictures, markings and other reproduction issues beyond our control. Because this work is culturally important, we have made it available as part of our commitment to protecting, preserving, and promoting the world's literature.

GUIDE TO FOLD-OUTS MAPS and OVERSIZED IMAGES

The book you are reading was digitized from microfilm captured over the past thirty to forty years. Years after the creation of the original microfilm, the book was converted to digital files and made available in an online database.

In an online database, page images do not need to conform to the size restrictions found in a printed book. When converting these images back into a printed bound book, the page sizes are standardized in ways that maintain the detail of the original. For large images, such as fold-out maps, the original page image is split into two or more pages

Guidelines used to determine how to split the page image follows:

• Some images are split vertically; large images require vertical and horizontal splits.
• For horizontal splits, the content is split left to right.
• For vertical splits, the content is split from top to bottom.
• For both vertical and horizontal splits, the image is processed from top left to bottom right.

List aaa.26,

TREATISE

ON

REGENERATION.

By PETER VAN MASTRICHT, *D.D.*
Profeſſor of Divinity in the Univeiſities of FRANCFORT,
DUISBURGH, and UTRECHT.

Extracted from his Syſtem of Divinity, called Theologia theoretico-practica; and faithfully tranf-
lated into Engliſh; With an APPENDIX,
containing Extracts from many celebrated Divines of the reformed Church, upon the fame
Subject.

NEW-HAVEN:

Printed and Sold by THOMAS and SAMUEL
GREEN, in the Old-Council-Chamber.

PREFACE.

THE reader will perhaps be defirous to know, who this Doct. *Van Maftricht* is, and what the particular reafons are, for publifhing the following Treatife at this time. The Publifher will endeavour, in brief to fatisfy the reader in both.

Peter Van Maftricht, author of the following Treatife; was born in the year 1630, in the city of *Cologn*, in *Germany*, of honorable parentage, many of whofe anceftors had been confiderable fufferers in the proteftant caufe. He was educated in the univerfity of *Utrecht*; was feveral years a preacher, in various parts of *Germany* and *Denmark*; was invited to fettle in *Copenhagen*, capital of the latter: But was prevailed upon by the *Elector* of *Brandenburg*, (grand-father, or great-grand-father to the prefent king of *Pruffia*) to accept the place of profeffor of Hebrew and practical divinity, in his new eftablifhed univerfity at *Francfort*. He afterwards ferved in the fame ftation at *Duifburg*, near his native place; and the laft thirty years of his life, he fuftained the fame office in the famous univerfity of *Utrecht*, the place of his education. He was greatly efteem'd as a moft accurate, judicious, learned and pious divine. He died in this office near eighty years of age. His fyftem of divinity, from whence the following Treatife is extracted, is the product of a long life, fpent in the ftudy, practice and inftruction of divinity.

The reafon for tranflating and publifhing the following Treatife at this time, is principally a hope, that it may have a tendency to put a ftop to the controverfy, which feems to be growing among us, relative to regeneration,

neration ; Whether it be wrought by the immediate influences of the divine Spirit, or by light as the means ? and happily to unite us in the truth. The tranflator is encouraged thus to hope, from the following confiderations,

1. He hath frequently heard gentlemen, who maintain oppofite fides of this queftion, manifeft their entire approbation of, and concurrence with *Van Maftricht* ; which induces him to think, that with many, the controverfy is more about terms than any thing elfe ; and that when they find, they both can agree with *VanMaftricht*, they will be lead fo to explain themfelves, as to agree with each other.

2. As our Author cannot be looked upon as partial in favour of any particular fyftem of doctrines prevailing amongft *us* ; 'tis hoped and expected that all will read him without prejudice or partiality.

3. The great character which our author fuftains, for which we have the ample teftimony of Dr. *Cotton Mather*, (whofe name hath always been much refpected in the churches of *New-England*) in the following words, ‡
" There is nothing that I can with fo much pleropho-
" rie recommend unto you, as a *Maftricht*, his *Theologia*
" *theoretico practica.* That a minifter of the gofpel may
" be thoroughly furnifhed unto every good work, and
" in one or two quarto volumns enjoy a well furnifhed
" library ; I know not that the fun has ever fhone up-
" on an human compofure that is equal to it ; and I
" can heartily fublcribe unto the commendation which
" *Pontanus*, in his *Laudatio Funebris* upon the author has
" given of it. *De hoc opere confidenter affirmo, quod eo or-*
" *dine fit digeftum, tanto rerum pondere prægnans et tumidum,*
" *tanta et tam varia eruditione refertum ; ut nefcio an in illo*
" *genere ufquamGentium exftet aliquid magis accuratum et ela-*
" *boratum.*

‡ Dr. Mather's directions for a Candidate of the miniftry. P. 85.

a boratum. † I hope you will, next unto the facred
" fcriptures, make a *Maftricht* the ftorehoufe to which
" you may refort continually. But above all things re-
" member the dying words of this true Divine ; which
" he uttered *altiffima voce* (with a loud voice, and I wifh
" all that ftudy divinity might hear it !) *Se nullo loco et*
" *numero habere veritatis defenfionem, quam fincera pietas*
" *et vitæ fanctitas, individuo nexu non comitetur.*" * The
character, I fay, of our Author, and his profeffedly de-
livering upon this point the general fentiment of the
whole reformed church abroad, it is hoped, will weigh
fo much, in the mind of every one, as to obtain a candid
examination of his fentiments, before they reject them.

4. Our Author's arguments are exceeding plain,
fcriptural, and convictive. There is nothing liable to
the imputation of metaphyfical nicety and fubtilty. So
far from it that his Contemporaries, who oppofed his
doctrines, " accufed him of not allowing reafon its proper place ; but of dethroning it thro' pretence of religion." 'Tis therefore to be hoped, that many who have
oppofed the fentiments which our Author maintains,
from a notion of their being metaphyfical fubtilties, will
by his plain, fcriptural arguments, be convinced of the
truth of them.

5. Many, 'tis to be feared, are prejudiced againft the
doctrine which our Author endeavours to eftablifh in
the following Treatife, from a notion that it is *new,* and
unheard of in the Chriftian Church. The following
Treatife,

---

† In Englifh thus. Of this work (i. e his fyftem of divinity) I
confidently affirm, that it is difpofed in that order, abounds in fuch
weighty matter, and is filled with fuch a copious variety of learning,
that I know not whether the world can afford any thing of the kind
better ftudied, and more accurate than this.

* That he hath no opinion of any defence of the truth, which
fincere piety and holinefs of life doth not infeperably accompany.

Treatife, it is hoped, will entirely remove this groundlefs objection.

But if this little Treatife fhould not prove fo fuccefsful, as to reconcile our differences upon this point, it will at leaft ferve this purpofe, to enable thofe, who have not opportunity, to look into antient authors on this fubject, to judge in fome meafure what the fentiments of the Reformed Church have been upon this important point.

Thefe confiderations induce the Tranflator ftrongly to hope, that this publication may be of happy fervice, at the prefent day. Should it in any meafure contribute to the promoting and maintaining of truth, the Tranflator will think himfelf amply rewarded for his trouble.

The Tranflator begs the candour of the Reader, with regard to the many inelegancies of ftile, which, he is apprehenfive, the critical reader will difcover in the following pages. Our Author's manner of writing is laconic, with very little decoration or ornament. A tranflation, in any meafure literal, muft refemble the genius of the original: And many Idioms of the original language will be apt infenfibly to flide into the tranflation. The Tranflator had rather forego any ornaments of ftile, which the work might receive from a more free tranflation, than thereby endanger himfelf to mifreprefent the fenfe of our Author. He hopes the Tranflation juftly reprefents the Author's fentiments, which he looks upon the principal thing; and therefore perfuades himfelf, that any little inaccuracies of expreffion, will be kindly overlooked by the benevolent reader.

ON

ON REGENERATION.

JOHN iii. 5.

Verily, verily I say unto thee, except a man be born of Water, and of the Spirit, he cannot enter into the Kingdom of God.

I. HAVING in a former treatise discoursed upon the *first* act of application, in which the holy Spirit *offers* to those who are to be saved, for their reception, the Redeemer and Redemption. I come now to discourse upon the *second*, in which he *bestows* upon them that *power*, by which they are *enabled* to receive the offered benefits; which is done by *regeneration*, the necessity of which our Saviour holds forth in the words above mentioned.

> The second act of application is regeneration

THE EXPLANATORY PART.

II. These words contain a weighty, powerful assertion of our Saviour, concerning the *necessity of regeneration*. In which we may note,

> The text explained.

1. *The person asserting.* I say unto you; I whom just now you saluted by the title of *Rabbi*, or Master, *a master sent from God*, of which you have been con-

B   vinced

ᵃ Ver. 2.
ᵇ Iſa. 65. 16.
ᶜ John 14. 6.
ᵈ Titus 1. 2.
Heb 6. 18.
ᵉ John 8. 14.
ᶠ John 3. 7.

vinced by ſo many miracles; ᵃ *I*, who am the *Amen*, ᵇ or the God of truth; ᵇ yea, the *truth* itſelf, ᶜ which cannot either deceive or be deceived; ᵈ whom therefore you may ſafely believe, *do aſſert*, *teſtify* and *declare* ᵉ unto you, and not only to you, but to the whole nation; yea, and to all generations which ſhall exiſt in future ages. ᶠ

2. *The manner of aſſertion, amen, amen, verily, verily.* The word *amen* is of Hebrew derivation, from the root, *aman* (to be ſtable or firm) which is retained in the Greek, Syriac, Arabic, and all the Latin verſions; and alſo in the vulgar languages. It is an adverb of *aſſerting*; that is *verily, certainly,* or the thing is ſo, or this is the *truth*. Aquila renders it, by *faithfully*; the Seventy by, *ſo be it*, but ſometimes retain the word *amen*. It is uſed either to *confirm* what hath been already ſpoken, ᵍ or to *affirm* what is now to be ſaid. The firſt uſe is moſt frequent in the old teſtament, the latter in the new. It is a particle uſed for confirmation, and is rendered either by *verily* or *ſo be it*: in the firſt ſenſe it is uſed in confirmation of ſomething *affirmed*, in the latter, in confirmation of ſomething *wiſhed* or *deſired*. If the ſentence be an *informative aſſertion*, the word means *verily or truly*; but if *optative* or intreative, the meaning is, *ſo be it.* The particle *nai* comprehends both ſignifications; as it is ſometimes *aſſertory*, ſometimes expreſſive of vehement deſire. Hence Luke uſeth the word *nai* (yea) for *amen*. The apoſtle Paul connects them together, ᵇ *yea and amen*; that one might emphatically explain the other. Our Saviour repeats the word *amen* (verily) perhaps in different ſenſes, ſo that the *firſt* may ſignify himſelf, I the *amen*, the *God of truth*; ⁱ as it is ſaid theſe things ſaith the *Amen, the faithful & true Witneſs*.ᵏ The *latter* may ſignify the truth of the thing aſſerted. So that the meaning of the expreſſion may be this, I the God of *truth* declare the *truth* unto you. It may also

ᵍ Num. 5. 22.
Deut 27 26
1 Cor. 14. 16.

ʰ 2 Cor. 1. 17.

ⁱ Iſ. 65. 16.

ᵏ Rev. 3: 14.

also be defigned to confirm and ftrengthen the truth of his paradox concerning the abfolute neceffity of regeneration, and the more powerfully to beget in Nicodemus a belief of the doctrine; I, the Mafter fent from God, verily fay unto you, and that repeated-ly. There are fome who think the repetition of the word denotes, not a fimple affirmation ; but an *oath*, and that it is the fame in fenfe with the expreffion, *as I live faith the Lord*, in the old teftament, as the Chaldee verfion, for this expreffion, hath, as I am *conftant*, ftable, firm, or as I am the *amen*, the God of truth. But it doth not appear to me confiftent, that one who fo feverely cenfures a rafh oath, [1] fhould fo frequently fwear himfelf; for it is faid that this expreffion is ufed fifty times by our Saviour. However, we may at leaft confider it as a *forcible* manner of expreffion, or as the Hebrews fay, as *a corroboration of his words*, admirably fuited to this paradox of the abfolute neceffity of regeneration.

3. The thing *afferted*, with regard to which we may note,

(1) The fubject, *regeneration*, or the new-birth, "*except a man be born*," the fame thing in ver. 2, is expreffed by being born *again*, or *from above*. The word *anothen* rendered *again*, fignifies fometimes, *again*, or the *fecond* time ; thus Nicodemus feems to have underftood it : [m] in which fenfe it occurs, Gal. 4. 9. And thus *Syrus* and *Nonnus* render it in this place. The apoftle Peter ufeth the word *anagenethenai* to be born again. [n] In other places the word fignifies *from above*, or *from heaven*. [o] Which it feems our Saviour defigned to intimate, by explaining the word *anothen* ufed in verfe 3, by the expreffion *of water and of the fpirit*, in verfe 5, or to be born fpiritually and from above, that is from heaven. What if we fhould connect thefe two fenfes together, as one is fubordinate to the other : fo that to be born *anothen* fignifies both

[1] Mat. 5. 33, 34.

[m] Ver. 4.

[n] 1 Pet. i. 3.
[o] Ver. 31. 19. 11. ſu. 1. 17. and 17.

to

to be born *from above*, that is spiritually and from heaven; and also *again*, or the second time? since that being born, which is from above, or of the Spirit, is a second birth, as it follows the first and natural birth, which is after the flesh. "*Except a man be born again*," our Saviour calleth it a *birth or being born*, to denote the *universal* amendment or renovation of man thereby: he intimates the necessity of a renovation, not of this or that particular part or faculty, but a total renovation of the whole man, which is a new or second birth, whereby he becomes a *new man*, a *new creature*, and walks in *newness of life.* [p] Of which more under the *doctrinal* part.

(2) The *origin* of *regeneration*, "*of water and the spirit.*" The particle *ek* rendered *of*, as is plain from the subject, denotes in this place, not the *material*, but the *efficient* cause, as it doth in many other places; [q] since neither water nor spirit are the matter out of which a spiritual regeneration is effected. *Water and spirit*, some consider as two different things; so that by *water* they understand the *instrumental*, and by *spirit*, the *principal* cause, because (as they suppose) the spirit, by water, effects regeneration. But they who are of this opinion are divided; some by water understand the Jewish baptisms or washings; with which the Jews, more especially the Pharisees, were wont to wash their proselytes, before their admission into the Jewish church; likewise their own hands, clothes, meat and even their bodies, of which mention is made in various places of the new testament; [r] to these, our Nicodemus, as he was a Pharisee, must have been accustomed. Others by *water* here, understand the sacramental water of *baptism*, by which they suppose the Spirit effects regeneration. And here again some suppose the baptismal water to be *directly* intended, as most of the Fathers; others, only by way of allusion. Others more rightly understand but one thing expressed,

marginal notes:
2 Cor. 5. 17.
Gal. 6. 15.
Rev. 21. 5.

Rom 11. 36.
Luke 1. 35.

Mark 7. 8.
Heb. 9. 10.
Mark 7. 4.

fed by two terms, as the *water* of the Spirit, or spiritual water, or rather the *Spirit* having the properties of water, which like water cleanseth in regeneration. For our Saviour doth not mean to lead Nicodemus to receive the facrament of baptifm, (which at that time was not inftituted, at leaft as an ordinary, univerfal facrament ;) but to feek the regeneration of the Holy Ghoft. [s] "He faved us by the wafhing of regeneration :" wherefore in the continuation of this difcourfe, our Saviour makes no further mention of water, but only of the *Spirit.* [t] I need not obferve that by *Spirit* here, is to be underftood the third perfon in the facred Trinity, with relation to the work of fpiritual *purification,* which is effected by regeneration and renovation. [u] · Tit. 3. 5. · Ver. 6, 7, 8. · Tit. 3. 5.

(§) The *neceſſity* of this regeneration, with regard to which, may be obferved,

[1] The *manner,* in which both the neceſſity, and univerfality of it are expreſſed, *"except a man be born."* *A man,* that is, every man, which extends the neceſſity to all and, *every one,* fo that not one individual can be excepted from this neceſſity. However lefs is expreſſed by this form of fpeech, than is intended. It means not only that *no one* can be faved without this regeneration ; but that *all* the regenerate fhall be favved. Not that regeneration (at leaft in it's limited fenfe) is the only thing required unto falvation; fince befides this, *converſion,* fanctification, &c. are neceſſary, in which the *power,* beftowed in regeneration, may be drawn forth into the actual exercifes of faith and repentance : but that all and every one, who is regenerated, will alfo be brought to *converſion,* fanctification, faith and repentance, and fo to falvation.

[2] *The uſe,* or the purpofe to which regeneration is fubfervient, viz. *"entering into the kingaom of God."* The *kingdom* of God here fignifies both the kingdom of *grace* upon earth, or the church, [w] that the perfon regenerated may become a true and living member thereof ; · Mah 4. Col. 4. 11.

ᶻLuke 14 15
and 2; 42.
ᵃ Luke 8. 10

thereof; and alfo the kingdom of *glory* in heaven; ᵇ with all things which pertain to both thefe kingdoms, ᵃ i. e. all fpiritual bleffings.

[3. The *poſſeſſion* and enjoyment of this kingdom, "*He cannot enter thereinto.* Ver. *3.* "*He cannot fee the kingdom of God* " Here regeneration is extended to the *power,* "*be cannot,* " the reafon of which is given in the following verfe, "*That, which is born of the fleſh,* that is by *natural* generation, is *fleſh,* or carnal, defiled with fin ; and that, which is *born* of the *ſpirit,* is *ſpirit,* or *ſpiritual* and faving. For regeneration, ſtrictly fo cal-

ᵃEph 2 2 5.

ed, finds man fpiritually *dead,* ᵃ into whom it infufeth the firſt act, or principle of the fpiritual *life;* by which he hath a *power* or ability to perform fpiritual exer-cifes. Therefore, without this, he *can* neither *fee* the kingdom of God, that is *mentally,* as he is blind, " *He perceiveth not the things of the ſpirit of God : for they are fooliſhneſs unto him, neither can be know them, becauſe they*

ᵇ 1 Cor 2 14.

are ſpiritually diſcerned." ᵇ Nor if he could *fee,* could he *enter* into the kingdom of God, as "*be is not ſubject to*

ᶜ Rom 8. 7.

the law of God," neither indeed *can be ;* ᶜ who alfo "*of*

ᵈ 2 Cor 3. 5

himſelf is not ſufficient to think any thing ſpiritually good." ᵈ Who therefore ſtands in abfolute need of *illumination* by regeneration, in order to his *feeing* the kingdom of heaven, and of a *renovation* of his will, in order to his willing to *enter* into it. Which power is after-wards excited in the exercifes of faith and repentance, in converfion and fanctification, whereby he *fees* the kingdom of God, and at the fame time *enters* into the fame.

THE DOCTRINAL PART.

That befides
the external
call, regene-
ration is alfo
neceffary to
the applicati-
on of redemp-
tion, which is
proved by the
fcriptures,

III. It is not fufficient to the application of re-demption, or a participation therein, that the Re-deemer and the redemption purchafed by him, be of-fered, by the external call of the gofpel, to thofe who are to be faved, for their reception, unlefs that pow-er be beftowed upon them, by regeneration, by which they

they may be enabled to receive the offered benefits.
For the Redeemer himself expresly denies that any
one, without regeneration, *can* either *see* spiritual objects, or approach them, by entering into the kingdom of God. Hence faith, by which alone Christ is
applied to us, and we made partakers of his redemp-
tion, is ascribed only to those who are *born of God.* e *John 1.12,13
And the apostle is even more express than this, who,
after that he had taught that the *kindness of God our
Saviour had appeared unto men,* viz. By the external call
of the gospel, adds, that he saved them, that is applied to them the *kindness* or redemption of the Savi-
or, by the washing of *regeneration,* and the *renewing of*   f Tit. 3 4, 5.
the Holy Ghost. f The same thing is held forth in all   g James 1. 18.
those texts of scripture, which ascribe our partaking of   1 Pet. 1 3. 23.
Christ's redemption, or our salvation, (1) In express   h Deut. 30. 6.
terms to *regeneration,* and the renewing of the Holy   Rom. 2. 29.
Ghost: g (2) To *circumcision of the heart:* h (3) to the   Col. 2. 11 13.
taking away of the heart of stone, and the *putting* with- i Ezek. 36. 26.
in us a heart of flesh, the giving of a *new* heart and a   and 11 19.
new spirit. i (4) To the creation of a *pure* heart. k   Jer. 32. 39. &
(5) To spiritual *drawing*; l unless you would choose   31 32 k Pf 51.
to refer that to the grace of conversion. (6) To the   12. Eph. 2 10.
illumination of the mind, m and *renewing* of the will. n and 4. 24.
(7) To a spiritual *resurrection* and *quickening.* o All   2 Cor. 5. 17.
which expressions are synonimous with regeneration,   l Cant. 1. 4.
signifying the same thing in different terms.   n John 6. 44.

IV. The foundation of this necessity lieth in the   m Eph. 1. 18.
universal, spiritual death of all the elect, by which they, Phil. 2. 13.
as well as reprobates, are by nature *dead* in sin; p have o Eph. 2. 5. 6.
an heart of *stone*; q an *uncircumcised* heart; r are blind in John 5 25.
their *minds*; s have their *wills* alienated from God, from And by rea-
the life of God, and from all spiritual and saving   son.
good; t and are therefore utterly insufficient to think   p Eph. 2. 1. 5.
even the least good thought; and consequently also   & v. 14 Luke
to receive, by a living faith, the Redeemer offered to   15. 24. Mat. 8.
them in the gospel, and the necessary terms of salva-   22 Ez 37 2, 3.
tion;   q Ezek. 36 26.
                                                           r Acts 7 51.
                                                           s 1 Cor. 2 14.
                                                           Eph. 4 17, 18.
                                                           t Eph. 4. 18, 19
                                                           u 2 Cor. 3. 5
                                                           Josh. 24. 19.

tion; unless, by regeneration, *power* be bestowed upon them in a new spiritual *life* by the Holy Ghost. However a man spiritually **dead** can *hear* spiritual truths, he can also, *grammatically* at least, *understand* what he hears; he can moreover approve in his judgment, at least *speculatively*, what he understands, and lastly he can in a general manner have some kind of *affection* towards what he approves. Nor doth the holy Spirit in the work of regeneration and spiritual quickening, treat with the elect, as with *flocks* or brutes; but as *rational* creatures, to whose reception, the Redeemer, with the terms of salvation, have been already offered by the external call; to the reception of which, the Spirit hath *invited* them by the most pressing motives. Yea it is possible that persons, as yet spiritually dead, may, if not by the powers which they are *naturally* possessed of; yet by the assistance of common grace, arrive to certain attainments, not accompanying salvation, * or that are not inseperably connected therewith. So that we are not to think, there is nothing to be done with the unregenerate. However, while they perform *all* these things, they do *nothing* at all, which is *spiritual*, or before nothing in a spiritual manner. ˣ

V. That we may attain to a more clear understanding of the *nature* of this regeneration, so necessary to salvation: we must carefully observe with regard to the *word*, that both the scriptures, and also divines use it, sometimes in a *larger* sense, to denote the *whole* operation of the Holy Ghost upon the souls of those who are to be saved; whereby they are brought into a state of grace; so that, besides the external call, it comprehends conversion, and even initial sanctification: In which sense practical divines lay down the *marks*, motives, and means of regeneration: Sometimes the word regeneration is used in a more *limited* sense, as distinguished from the external call, from conversion

* Heb. 6. 4, 5.
6. 9

ˣ 1 Cor 2. 13, 14.
The meaning of the word regeneration.

conversion and from sanctification: So that the *external call* signifies only the *offer* of redemption for our reception: *Regeneration* conveys that *power* into the soul, by which the person, who is to be saved, is *enabled* to receive the offer: *Conversion* puts forth the power received into *actual* exercise, so that the soul doth *actually* receive the offered benefits: Sanctification brings forth the fruits of conversion, or of faith and repentance, in a carefulness to maintain good works; yet not so immediately, but that an union with Christ and justification come between conversion, and sanctification, at least in the order of nature, if not of time. It is in this *stricter* sense of the word, we shall consider the doctrine of regeneration at present. In which sense it means the same with *circumcision* of the heart, with *taking away* the heart of *stone*, and *putting* within us a heart of *flesh*, with a new *creation*, with *drawing*, with *illumination*, with *turning* the will, and especially with a spiritual *resurrection* and *quickening*, of which we have already spoken in sect. III. The terms used in Greek for regeneration are, *anakainosis*,[a] *agiasmos pneumatos*, [b]*kainee ktisis*, [c] *paliggenesia*, [d] *anageneesis*. [e] Thus regeneration, in the proper sense of the word, is only a *second* and spiritual *generation*, in which the *soul* receives its *spiritual life*, as the body receives it's *natural life* from the first generation. The *father* in this case is God; hence we are said to be *born* of God; [f] and the regenerate are called the *sons of God*. [g] The *mother* in whose womb as it were we are conceived and nourished, is the church.[h] The *seed, the word of God, which liveth and abideth forever*; [i] received by the external call of the gospel. From all which considerations, since a *divine nature* is communicated to the regenerate, similar in ts kind to the holiness of the Deity, it is with sufficient propriety called a generation, as that is only a ommunication of life, with a resemblance to the Father begetting.

Expressions synonimous with regeneration.

[a] 1 Tim. 3 5.
[b] 2 Thes 2 13
[c] 2 Cor. 5. 17.
[d] Mat. 19 28.
[e] 1 Pet. 1. 3. 23

[f] John 1. 13.
[g] 1 Joh. 5. 1, 2.

[h] Gal. 4. 26.
[i] 1 Pet. 1. 23.

What the
thing is, in-
tended by re-
generation.

VI As to the *thing* intended by regeneration; it is
only that *physical* † operation of the Holy Ghost,
whereby he begets in men who are elected, redeemed
and

† The word, *physical*, which is frequently used by our author, is
offensive to some gentlemen, who seem not to reject the thing intended by it their dislike thereto seems to arise from an apprehen-
sion that it implies the bestowment of a new natural faculty such as
the understanding, will, or affections: but this 'tis evident is not our
author's meaning and perhaps not the meaning of any, who use
the term. They do not suppose the regenerate to exercise any natural facul y which the unregenerate do not. They use the word
simply in opp fi ion to *moral*. Now a *moral* operation is the effec-
ting of some hig by moral suasion or by the laying of arguments
and inducements before the mind : but these, however great and
strong, attended with never so much light in the understanding,
our author supposes, will not effect regeneration : but supposes there
is a positive, immediate act of the divine spirit upon the soul, infusing a new principle of spiritual and divine life ; whereby the
soul is enabled, or qualified to exercise its natural powers and faculties in a spiritual manner. Some have chosen to express themselves hereupon in this form, viz That God in regeneration acts
after the manner of a physical cause, as Dr Ames, Rutherford, &c.
and the same thing, I take it, is intended by our English Divines
when they call that operation, which regenerates, *supernatural.*
They certainly use this word in opposition to *moral*, or any operation by moral suasion, or the laying of arguments and motives before the mind See extracts from Ridgly, Willard, &c in the appendix -- Indeed, 'till of late, scarce any, but Pelagians, denied
what is intended by a physical operation in regeneration, and the
word *physical* has generally been made use of : tho' some have re-
stricted the physical operation of the spirit in regeneration to the
understanding, as most of the *Arminians*, and some of the *reformed*,
who have held to regeneration by an illumination of the understanding ; they seem to have been influenced to this restriction,
thro' fear, least, if they ex ended the *physical* operation to the *will*,
the freedom of man's will could not be maintained But, tho' the
generality of the reformed call the regenerating act of God a physical operation ; yet I no where find, that they call the *change*,
that is wrought in man thereby, a *physical change*. The immediate
term or effect of regeneration according to Van Mastricht is, (§ x.
xi. xii) *grace*, spiritual life, &c. which is a moral change in the
m n, or a change of the moral state of his mind , tho' wrought by
a physical operation Nor is there any thing absurd in this, that
the operation should be *physical*; and yet the effect *moral* : for none
would suppose it beyond the power of God, (if he is pleased to exercise

and externally called, the *first act* or the principle of spiritual life, by which they are enabled to receive the offered Redeemer, and comply with the conditions of salvation. From this description may come into consideration,

VII. First. The *Author* of regeneration, which is God absolutely considered; [k] that *Father of Lights*, from whom cometh down every *good and perfect gift*; [l] because regeneration is a transient act, common to the whole Trinity; hence in the œconomy of redemption, it is attributed, (1) To the Father, as most agreeable to the character of a *father* which he sustains, [m] *from whom all the family in heaven and earth is named,* [n] who therefore as he begat his *own* Son, so he also begets us; so that he is both his and our Father. [o] A gain,

The Author of regeneration.
k John 1 13.
Eph 2 5
l Jam. 1 17, 18
m 1 Pet 1 3.
Jam 1 17, 18.
n Eph. 3. 15.
o John 20. 17.

ercise it) to determine the will of man to some particular volition, otherwise, than by arguments or motives, (this is before a possible case; here the operation would be *physical*, and yet the effect *moral*. So that the supposition of a *physical* operation, and yet a *moral* change as the effect of it, is not inconsistent in itself. And that this is actually the case, we trust our author hath sufficiently proved. The word *principle* which is here used for the immediate effect of this physical operation, and which is frequently used in this translation, has likewise given offence to some, as being a thing entirely unintelligible, a strange *something*, or a sort of *substratum* in the soul, which lies beyond the reach of human knowledge. 'Tis confessed it cannot be explained otherwise than by its consequences or effects. And is not the soul an *unknown* substratum of cogitation, whose existence can be known only by its operations? and what are the *faculties* of the soul, the *understanding*, *will* and *affections*, but *unknown* substrata of their several exercises? and what is matter but an *unknown* substratum of extension, solidity, &c. and what are all habits, but unknown substrata of their exercises? these substrata are unknown as to the nature of them. Their existence is known only by the qualities or actions they support. But who will disbelieve their existence, because they cannot fully comprehend the abstract nature of them? the implantation of a principle or substratum of holy exercises in regeneration is argued and known from its exercises, and operations. And we can tell the nature of it, as well as we can the nature of matter, of the soul, the faculties of the soul, and the like. And when these latter are explained, we shall think ourselves obliged to explain the former, or disbelieve its existence, but not before.

gain, (2) Regeneration is ascribed to the *Son*, as the *meritorious* cause,[p] who for this reason is stiled a *quickening spirit*,[q] and the life, which we live, we are said to *live* by the faith of the *Son* of God.[r] And (3) To the Holy Ghost;[s] hence he is stiled the *spirit of life*;[t] because the Holy Spirit by his operation *immediately* effects regeneration : and the spiritual life is with peculiar propriety ascribed to the *spirit of life.* The *moving* cause is merely God's *great love*,[u] his *abundant mercy*,[w] his gracious *good pleasure.*[x] Nor is there, especially before regeneration, (while we are the children of *wrath, dead* in sin[a]) any thing in us which can in the least merit such a favour. The *instrument* of regeneration, (but that merely of a *moral* kind) is the word of God,[b] previously offered and received in the external call of the gospel, as we have already observed.

VIII. *Secondly*, we may consider the *subjects* of regeneration, which are, (1) *Men*, who are endowed with understanding and will, to whom, agreeably to their *rational* nature, the Spirit hath previously *offered* redemption for their reception ; with whom therefore, he is pleased to treat, not as with stocks or brutes, as we have already observed. (2) They are the *elect* ;[c] for regeneration is not a common gift ; but a gift proceeding from the most *distinguishing* or special grace, as it flows from God's *great* love,[d] from his *abundant* mercy.[d] (3) They are *redeemed* ; hence Peter speaks of regeneration, as peculiar to those, who are *sprinkled with the blood of Christ*[e] Again, (4) They are such, who are as yet *dead in sin* :[f] for unless a man be dead, he cannot be made alive by regeneration. I add, (5) The *whole* man throughout,[g] is the subject of regeneration ; the understanding, will, affections, sensitive faculties, &c. that all may be quickened and renewed thereby.[h] As by natural generation, *all* the parts of a man are quickened or made alive ; and as, by sin, the *whole* man is become corrupt and dead.[i]

IX.

Marginal references:

P 1 Pet· 1.2.3.
q 1 Cor.15 45
r Gal 2 20 compared with Phil. 1 21 Col 3 4 John 14 6
s John 3 3 5 Tit 3 5
t Rom 8 2 10.
u Eph 2.5.6
w Pet 1 2 3. Tit. 3 5.
x Jam 1 17.
a Eph. 2 1,5.
b 1 Pet. 1.23.

The subjects of regeneration.

c 1 Pet 1 2 3 & chap 2 9
u Eph. 2. 5.
d 1 Pet. 1. 2,3.
e 1 Pet. 1 2,3
f Eph. 2 1 5 6
g 1 Thess 5 23
h 2 Cor 5 7
i Isa 1. 5 6.

IX. *Thirdly,* we may confider regeneration *itfelf,* or the regenerating *act.* Which certainly, is not a moral act, exercifed in offering and inviting, as is the cafe with the *external call.* But it is a *phyfical* act powerfully infufing fpiritual life into the foul : Which is proved. not only, (1) By the conftant phrafeology of the *fcriptures,* when they fpeak of the *exceeding greatnefs of his power towards thofe who believe, according to the working of his mighty power,* or the *energy* of the power of his might ; yea the fame power which was exerted in raifing *Chrift* from the dead. [k] Which expreffions certainly do not befpeak a *moral* agency. Alfo where the fcriptures fpeak of fpiritual *circumcifion,* of taking away the heart of ftone, of putting within us a heart of flefh, of creating a new heart, of drawing, of working in us to will and to do, of a *refurrection* from the dead, of which we have fpoken in fect. III. Do thefe expreffions in the leaft favour an operation merely *moral?* But, (2) It may alfo be proved by the very nature of the thing, in as much as regeneration is an operation upon men fpiritually *dead,* infufing life into them ; [l] but what moral operation, in teaching offering, perfuading, can be rationally exercifed upon a man that is *dead?*

X. The *term* of this phyfical operation, or the firft and immediate *effect* of regeneration, is varioufly expreffed in fcripture. *Firft,* it is fometimes called *grace,* [m] as *I will pour out the fpirit of grace ;* i. e. I will pour out *grace* by my Spirit. *Be thou ftrong in the grace that is in Chrift Jefus ;* [n] and in other places to the like purpofe. By which *grace* we do not here underftand, (1) The free *kindnefs* of God, which is called *grace freely giving,* *(gratia gratis dans)* and external grace ; from which not only *man,* but every *creature,* receiveth whatever good he poffeffeth. By which alfo a man already regenerate, and poffeffed of fpiritual power, thro' a gracious providental influence, is excited to exert in *fpiritual*

The act of regeneration.

[k] Eph. 1. 19. 20.

[l] Eph. 2. 1. 5. 6

The term of immediate effect of regeneration.
1. Grace.
[m] Zach. 12. 1
[n] 2 Tim. 2.
Heb. 13
1 Pet. 2.

ritual operations, the power he hath received. But, (2) By grace we here underſtand the *effect* of this kindneſs *grace, freely given, (gratia gratis data)* or *internal* grace, which in the ſcriptures is called *chariſma* ° (the free gift.) Nor, (3) Do we underſtand by grace here *every* effect of this kindneſs, ſince all the good which every creature enjoyeth, and even the whole creation, is from the *grace* of God, and in this ſenſe univerſal grace may be allowed : But we underſtand that grace which is contradiſtinguiſhed to *nature*, and as it exiſts in man, to the natural powers of *free will.* Neither, (4) Do we underſtand hereby *every* effect of grace, by which one man in his kind excells another. *v. g* The gift of mechanical *ſkill*, ᵖ or wiſdom in civil government, which may be called *common* grace, by the aſſiſtance of which, in things of a *moral* nature, a man may perform any of thoſe things which are not (as the apoſtle ſays) *echomena ſoterias*, or that have not a neceſſary connection with eternal ſalvation : But, (5) By *grace*, we here underſtand that effect of God's kindneſs, or the chariſma (free gift) by which one man hath power to perform ſpiritual exerciſes, while another hath it not ; and ſuch exerciſes, indeed to which God hath promiſed eternal ſalvation; which to uſe the apoſtle's words, do accompany ſalvation (echomena ſoterias.ᵠ) Finally in this ſenſe, by the grace beſtowed in regeneration, we underſtand that ſupernatural *power*, by which a man is enabled to comply with the conditions of the covenant of grace, to apprehend the Redeemer by a living *faith*, to come up to the terms of ſalvation, to repent of ſin, to love God and the Mediator ſupremely, &c.

XI. *Secondly*, the term or immediate effect of regeneration, is more frequently called *ſpirit.* ʳ *That which is born of the fleſh, is fleſh, and that which is born of the ſpirit, is ſpirit;* ˢ from which the regenerate are ſtiled *ſpiritual*, ᵗ who are *ſpiritually minded;* ᵘ (*phronema tou pneumatos.*

Margin notes:
ᵒRom. 12 6.
& ch 1 11
1 Cor 1. 7.

ᵖExod. 31 2. 3

Heb. 6. 9.

Spirit.
John 3 16.
Gal 5. 16,
18. 22.
Gal. 6 1.
Cor. 3. 1
Rom. 8. 7.

matos) *who perceive the things of the spirit and spiritually* [w] 1 Cor. 2. 14.
difcern them. [w] By the word fpirit here we underftand
not the Spirit *giving*; but the fpirit *given*, that is the
fpirit, which the Holy Ghoft beftows in regeneration,
the prefence of which makes the foul *fpiritually* alive,
as much as the prefence of the animal fpirit makes the
body *naturally* alive.[a] Hence this fpirit is faid to quick-
en or make alive, [b] therefore it is ftiled the fpirit of
life, [c] becaufe the prefence of this fpirit, which is *im-*
planted in the foul, conftitutes the *fpiritual* life, and
capacitates and inclines the man to *fpiritual* exercifes,
juft as the natural fpirit doth to *natural* exercifes. This
fpirit, beftowed by the Holy Ghoft in regeneration,
is, according to it's various exercifes, ftiled fometimes
the *fpirit of grace*, fometimes the *fpirit of prayer*, [d] the
fpirit of faith, [e] &c. agreeably to that virtue and ope-
ation which it produces in the regenerate. So that
by the fpirit here we underftand only that *fpiritual*
power, by which we are enabled to perform *fpiritual*
exercifes in a fpiritual *manner*. By *fpiritual* exercifes
or fpiritual things we mean the fame as the apoftle by
the things of the fpirit, [f] and our Saviour, by *the bufinefs*
or the things of his Father. [g]

[a] Ezek. 37. 5.
Acts 20. 10.
[b] John 6. 63.
[c] Rom. 8. 2.

[d] Zach. 12. 10.
[e] 2 Cor. 4. 13.
compared
with Ifaiah
11. 1, 2.

[f] 1 Cor. 2. 14.
[g] Luke 2. 49.

XII. *Thirdly*, the term, or immediate effect of re- 3. Life.
generation, is more clearly called fpiritual *life*, in its
rft act (or principle,) from which God is faid to *quick-*
en, together with Chrift, thofe who are dead in fin, [h]
that we may be *raifed* together with him in a fpiritual
manner. [i] From the want of which fpiritual life, the
unregenerate are faid to be *dead* in fin, alienated from
he *life of God*; [k] and from the prefence of which, on
he other hand, we are faid *to live to God*, [x] to the *will*
of God, and *according* to God. [l] This fpiritual life confifteth in a *reunion* of the divine image, or original
righteoufnefs with our fouls, by which our firft parents,
in a ftate of innocence, were enabled to *live* to God,
and were difpofed to all fpiritual exercifes. [m] For as

[h] Eph. 2. 5.

[i] Col. 3. 1.

[k] Eph. 4. 18.
[x] Gal. 2. 20.
[l] 1 Pet. 4. 2. 6.

[m] Eph. 4. 24.
the Col. 3. 10.

the *natural* life confifteth in the *union* of the foul with the body ; fo the *fpiritual* life confifteth in the union of original righteoufnefs with the foul. And as a man hath power to perform all *natural* actions from the *natural* life, fo from .he fpiritual life the regenerate have power to perform all *fpiritual* exercifes. And laftly, as in the natural life, are virtually contained all a man's *natural powers*, which afterwards, by organs properly difpofed, come forth into action : fo in this fpiritual life, are virtually contained all thofe *fpiritual* graces, which, by the influence of converting grace, are in due time drawn forth by degrees into actual exercife.

XIII. Hence *fourthly*, the immediate effect of regeneration is alfo called the *feed* of God. [g] Becaufe in the *grace*, in the *fpirit*, and in the fpiritual *life*, which are beftowed upon the elect in regeneration, are contained the feeds of all thofe graces, which are neceffary to falvation : Which, under proper circumftances, do, by the heavenly dews of converting grace, gradually, yet with abfolute certainty, in due time, put forth their bloffoms and fruit in *actual* exercife ; like as the feeds of vegetables buried in the earth, when watered by genial fhowers, fhoot forth into the ftalk, flowers and fruit. And, *fifthly*, this immediate effect is called a *new creature*, [h] from which the regenerate are ftiled the *workmanfhip* of God, *created in Chrift Jefus unto good works, that they might walk in them.* [i] Alfo, *fixthly, it is* called a *new heart* and a *new fpirit*, [k] becaufe thereby the whole regenerate man, and all that is his, *fpirit* or underftanding, *heart* or will, all are *renewed*, [l] from which there is born a *new* man. [m] Thus far concerning the general term, or the firft and immediate effect of regeneration, which is the *fpiritual life* in its *firft* act (or principle,) which is alfo called by other names, as *grace,* the *fpirit, the feed of God, a new creature,* &c.

XIV.

Marginal notes:

[g] The feed of God.
1 John 3 9.

[h] A new creature.
2 Cor. 5. 7.
Gal. 6 17.
Eph. 2. 10.
Ezek 36.25.

[i] 2 Cor 5.17.
Thef 5. 23.
Eph. 4 23.
Col. 3, 10.

XIV. This fpiritual life, animating and quickening the *whole* regenerate man, and all the feveral parts and faculties of him, hath different *names* according to thofe different faculties. As it takes place in the *underftanding* it is called a *new fpirit,* [n] and fpiritual *light,* [o] and the beftowment of it by regeneration is called *illumination,* [p] and thofe who are illuminated are called *children of the light* ; [q] are faid to *walk in the light* of the Lord, [r] which light begets in them the *knowledge of the glory of God in the face of Chrift Jefus our Lord,* [s] and alfo the faving *knowledge* of God, [t] and the Mediator. [u] This fpiritual light of the regenerate effects, (1) The fimple *underftanding* or perception, [w] by which they know fpiritual objects, not only fpeculatively as true, but practically as good. (2) It affects the *judgment,* fo that the regenerate judge concerning the goodnefs of fpiritual things, not only as to the general pofition (*in thefi,*) what is good in a general view ; but alfo under all the particular circumftances and connections of that truth (*in hypothefi,*) what is good and profitable for them at this very time, all circumftances confidered. [x] In the meantime, this faving illumination in regeneration, is to be cautioufly diftinguifhed from the illumination, which is given in the external call, [z] in which fpiritual light is rather held up to view, than conveyed [a] into the foul; or if fome degree of light be beftowed by an internal work, [b] that however is either merely *fpeculative,* extorting only an acknowledgement and profeffion of the truth, [c] or if it be practical alfo, is fo only (*in thefi*) or reprefenting only, in a general manner, the goodnefs of the truth acknowledged by him: [d] But not (*in hypothefi*) under all the circumftances of it, fo as to excite a love to the truth, [e] or engage us in obedience thereto, fo as to walk in it ; [f] but is rather holding the truth in unrighteoufnefs. [g]

XV. As this fpiritual life, beftowed in regeneration, is feated in the *will,* it is ftiled *a new heart,*

D

Marginal notes:

Regeneration of the underftanding, called illumination.

[n] Eph. 4. 23.
Rom. 12. 2.
[o] Eph. 5. 8.
[p] Eph. 1 18.
2 Cor. 4. 6.
[q] Luke 16 18.
Eph. 5 8
1 Thef. 5 5.
[r] Ifa. 2 5
[s] 2 Cor. 4. 6.
Col. 3. 10.
[t] John 17 3.
[u] Ifa. 53 2.
[w] 1 Cor. 2. 14.

[x] Pf. 73. 28.

[z] Heb. 6 4.
[a] John 1. 5.

[b] Num. 24 3
[c] Mat 7 21 22
Rom 2. 17—
23 [d] Mar. 13
20, 21. Heb
6 4, [f] 2 Thef
2. 19 [e] Gal. 2
14 & ch 3 1
[g] Rom. 1. 18

Regeneration of the will.

h Pſal 51 12.
Ezek 36 2'.
i Jer 32 39
o Heb 3 10
Ezek 11 19.
20.

m Rom. 2.14.
15 n Luke 18
10, 1, 12
Phi, 3 5 6
o Mark 9 19.
20, 21 Heb.
6 4 5

p Eph 2 1 5.
q 2 Cor. 3 5.

r Rom 7 22.
2 Theſ 3 5

heart, [h] *a heart of fleſh,* or a heart eaſily affected, [i] a heart on which God hath *written his fear,* [k] by which the regenerate *walk in his ſtatutes.* [l] For the Holy Ghoſt implants in the *heart* or will, by regeneration, a new *inclination* or propenſity towards ſpiritual good. For altho' the will hath naturally a kind of propenſity toward *moral* good in general, [m] and toward *external* religious duties, [n] whereby, in duties, *with which ſalvation is not connected,* an unregenerate perſon may ſometimes perform things really wonderful : [o] Yet, their propenſity towards ſpiritual and *ſaving* good, mankind have utterly loſt by ſin ; hence they are ſaid to be *dead* in ſin, [p] and inſufficient to think even the leaſt thought ſpiritually good. [q] Wherefore it is abſolutely neceſſary, that a new *propenſity* toward *ſpiritual* good, be reſtored to the will. [r] For altho' the will doth naturally follow the *laſt* dictate of the practical underſtanding, ſo that, were the *underſtanding* but ſufficiently illuminated, an immediate renovation of the will might ſeem unneceſſary ; yet this is to be admitted for truth, only when the underſtanding, in its laſt dictate, judgeth agreeably to the *inclination* of the will. For that is *good,* with reference to the will, which is agreeable to its propenſity. So that, if we ſhould make the abſurd ſuppoſition of the *underſtanding's* being moſt clearly enlightened, and yet the *will* not renewed, the will would not follow the practical judgment, becauſe in that caſe the underſtanding would not dictate agreeably to it's propenſity. v. g. If David's underſtanding dictated, that chaſtity at this very time, all circumſtances conſidered, ought to be choſen by him, rather than adultery ; yet whilſt his underſtanding dictateth not agreeably to the preſent *propenſity* of his will, which inclineth to adultery, the will would by no means follow the laſt dictate of the underſtanding It is therefore in this ſpiritual propenſity of the will that the ſeeds of all thoſe graces, which are neceſſary to falvation are contained : Hence the *feed* of the regenerate is faid to remain in them, by reafon of which they cannot *abandon* themfelves to fin. [a]

XVI. Nor is the *fpiritual life*, in regeneration, beftowed only upon the *fuperior* faculties of the foul, the underftanding and will : But alfo upon the *inferior* or fenfitive faculties ; the affections, fenfes, and even the members of the body. Hence the apoftle exprefly afcribes fanctification not only to *the fpirit*, by which he feems to underftand the fpiritual faculties, fuch as agree to fpirits only, as the underftanding and will : but alfo to the *foul*, (*Pfuche*, properly the animal foul, from which we are called *pfuchikoi*, natural or fenfual, as it is rendered,) which denotes the inferior faculties fuch as are common to brutes ; yea, he extends fanctification even to the body and members of the body. [t] For as by fin a fpiritual *death* and *irregularity* are bro't upon thefe faculties, whereby they ftrive againft the fpirit : [u] Which irregularity is exprefly reprefented as criminal by the Holy Spirit, (1) As it takes place in the *affections* or paffions of the foul, [x] (2) In the *fenfitive* faculties v. g. *feeing* [w] and *hearing*, [a] (3) In the bodily *members*, [b] &c ; Therefore a fpiritual life, by regeneration, muft be reftored to thefe faculties, to enable them rightly to difcharge their refpective fervices. [c] This life in the *inferior* faculties is a *difpofition* to *obedience*, whereby they become fitted not to oppofe the fpirit, or underftanding and will; but to be in fubjection to, or to be led by the *fpirit*. [d] As at firft, in a ftate of integrity, by our original righteoufnefs, which confifted in the divine image, thofe inferior faculties were moft beautifully arranged under the government of the mind.

XVII. The fpiritual life is beftowed by regeneration, only in the *firft act* (or principle) not in the *fecond acts* (or operation,) underftood either as *habits* or *exercifes*. For as, by *natural* generation, a man receives

neither

[a] 1 John 3. 9.

Regeneration in the inferior faculties.

[t] 1 Thef 5 23.

[u] Gal 5. 17.

[w] Rom. 5. 7
Gal 5. 24.
Col. 3. 5.
1 Thef. 4 5
Rom. 1 26
[x] 2 Pet. 2 14
[a] Pfal 58 5
[b] Rom 6. 19
and 3 13,14
15, 16
[c] Rom. 6. 10
[d] Gal. 5. 17,
Rom 6 12 14 17 Jam 1. 20.

Regeneration confers the fpiritual life in the firft act only.

neither the habits or acts of reasoning, speaking, or writing, but only the *power*, which under proper circumstances, in due time, comes forth into act : So also, in regeneration, there is not bestowed upon the elect, any *faith*, hope, love, repentance, &c. either as to habit or act ; but the *power* only of performing these exercises, is bestowed ; by which, the regenerate person doth not as yet actually believe, or repent ; but only is *capacitated* thereto · Wherefore the unregenerate are emphatically said, to be *unable*, either *to see*, as referring to the understanding, or *to enter*, referring to the will, into the kingdom of God. ᵉ Which power, in conversion, which succeeds regeneration, proper circumstances being supposed, is, in due time, brought into *actual* exercise. So that one *truly* regenerate may, both as to habit and act, be for a time an unbeliever, destitute of repentance and walking in sin   As appears, more clear than the light of the sun, in the instances of these, who are regenerated in their mothers wombs, or at their baptism, as Jeremiah, ᶠ John the baptist, ᵍ and Timothy, ʰ who nevertheless did not, till they arrived to the years of discretion, perform the actual exercises of faith or repentance. So that *regeneration*, in which the spiritual life is bestowed in the *first* act or principle only, differs from conversion, by which this principle of life is brought into *actual* exercise, not only in order of *nature* ; but sometimes also in order of *time*. However we mean not to deny here, that it may be, and often is the case, that a sanctification of the spirit, in a *general* sense, comprehending vocation, regeneration, conversion & sanctification properly so called, is effected at one and the same time : Which seems to have been the case with the thief on the cross, converted by Christ in his last moments.ⁱ We only mean that they *may* be seperated as to time, and that oft times this is *actually* the case.

ᵉ John 3. 3. and 5.

ᶠ Jer. 1. 5. ᵍ Luke 1 15 ʰ 2 Tim 3 15

ⁱ Luke 23 40. —44.

XVIII

XVIII. Since therefore regeneration conveys the spiritual life, in the *first* act or principle ; it may be easily determined. 1. That in regeneration a man is merely *passive,* as in the first reception of a natural life, the subject of it can be only *merely passive.*[k] For if he *did* any thing toward begetting life in himself ; he must be already *alive,* since a dead person cannot act ; and if already *alive,* then surely life is not begotten in him.

The affections of regeneration. 1 A man is entirely passive therein.

[k] John 1. 43. with Eph. 2. 5, 6.

XIX. 2. We may determine what ought to be held as to a *preparation* for regeneration : For there may two kinds of preparation come under consideration here ; *one,* which is supposed to proceed from the *person* to be regenerated, whereby, he prepares himself to receive regeneration ; or by the power of his own free will he becomes more disposed and prepared for regeneration than others. This, without the plainest contradiction, can by no means be admitted ; since regeneration is an operation upon a man spiritually *dead,* into whom the first act or principle of spiritual life is infused : Now, if he prepared himself thereto, he doubtlesly must do it by a previous principle of *life,* and so must be supposed alive, before life is implanted in him. The *other* kind of preparation is supposed to proceed from *God,* the author of regeneration. And again, this preparation, which is the work of God, may respect regeneration, either as taken in a *larger* sense, as denoting conversion also, and the term or immediate end of it, viz. Faith and actual repentance, in which conversion terminates : That God useth many preparatory means to regeneration, taken in this sense, by the help of which one may attain to this faith and repentance, we shall endeavour to shew, by divine assistance, in a *future* discourse : Or this preparation may respect regeneration in a more limitted sense, as denoting only the introduction of the first act or principle of spiritual life. Nor, in this sense,

2. How far regeneration admits of any preparation.

can

can any preparation, truly and properly so called, be admitted, any more than took place in the resurrection of Lazarus to a natural life.[1] If, however, you chuse to admit here *some kind* of preparation in those, who are to be made the subjects of this spiritual life, such, for instance, as in drying wood, which is to be set on fire, such also as God used in the work of creation, when he created on the first day a shapeless mass, which he formed and modified in the following days, and such as he peculiarly used in the creation of man, forming first the body of clay, or the rib, into which he afterwards breathed *the breath of life.*[m] I say, if in this sense you chuse, with many orthodox Divines, to admit some *preparation*, which is the work of God, I have no great objection thereto : And then this preparation may consist in the previous external call, so far as God, by the offers of grace, enlightens the mind of the person, who is to be regenerated, concerning the nature of redemption, and the terms of salvation, and invites him to embrace the same.

XX. 3. We may hence determine, that regeneration is *irresistable*, and in what sense this is to be understood. For if you consider what the person, who is to be regenerated is, *a child of wrath, dead in sin ;* he hath certainly depravity enough to resist : [n] But if you consider, that it is God, who regenerates and quickens, the subject of regeneration can no more *resist* God, than Lazarus of old *could* have resisted Christ, when raising him to a natural life.[o] Nor hath he *a will to* resist, for, by the spiritual life instantaneously produced, all inclination or desire of resisting is suppressed or taken away.[p]

XXI. 4. That the grace of regeneration, can never be *lost*, and the grounds upon which this *Inamissibility* is founded.[q] In this indeed, it differs from the *first* spiritual life, effected in creation, by the bestowment of original righteousness ; through the loss of which

by

Marginal notes:

[1] John 11. 43.

[m] Gen. 2. 7.

3 In what sense regeneration is irresistible.
[n] Acts 7 51.
Jo 11. 43 44
Ezek 36 25
26, 27. Jer
32 39, 40.
compare Gal.
. 13 Acts 9
—6, & 22 5
with v. 10. &
26. 9, 10 14.
with ver. 19

4. In what sense regeneration is inamissible.
[q] 1 John 3 9
Ezek 36. 27.
11 19 20.
Jer. 32. 39, 40

by fin, our firft Parents became *fpiritually dead ;* fince   *Eph. 2. 1.5.*
the fpiritual life beftowed by regeneration is never
entirely loft. However, the unfailing permanency of
this life is by no means to be afcribed to the *firmnefs*
and conftancy of the regenerate, or the *ftrength and*
perfection of the fpiritual life ; for there is, and always
dwells, in the regenerate, fo much corruption, that
they are as likely, by their own conduct, to deftroy
this life, as our firft parents were ; and indeed more
fo, becaufe they, before the lofs of their fpiritual life,
were *perfectly* righteous and holy.' But the impoffi-   *Eccl. 7. 29.*
bility of loofing the grace of regeneration depends,   *Rom 11.29.*
(1) On the grace of election and of the divine purpofe,   Math. 24.22.
hence the gifts and calling of God are without repen-   John 10. 28,
tance.' And, (2) Upon *preferving* grace."   29.

    XXII. 5. That this fpiritual life, as conveyed in   5. In what
regeneration, is but very *imperfect*, it being *only* the   fenfe it is im-
firft act or principle of fpiritual life, and only the *feeds*   perfect.
of fpiritual graces, which gradually like the feeds
of vegetables, grow up into the ftalk, bloffoms and   *1 Pet. 2 2*
fruit. Hence the regenerate, merely as fuch, are ftiled   *1 Cor. 3.1.*
new born babes," *babes in Chrift,*" who ftill have need to   Heb 5 12.
be nurfed, and indeed with food fuited to the infantile   13, 14.
ftate :" *That they may grow and wax ftrong in the fpirit,*   Luke 1. 80
as is faid of John the baptift ;° that is, in order that
the *firft* act or principle of life, conveyed in regeneration, might, by converfion, be drawn forth into actual
faith and repentance, which are the *fecond* acts or operations, and, if I may fo fay, the *branches* of this life :
And at length by *fanctification,* produce all thefe good   Gal. 5. 2
works, which are the fruits of the fpirit.' This fpiritual life is indeed fo fmall, that it cannot be well
known and diftinguifhed, but by its growth and *exer-*
cifes ; as *habits* cannot indeed be otherwife known,
than by their *Operations.*

THE ARGUMENTATIVE PART.

    XXIII. The moft of the controverfies on this fub-   Q 1, Wheth
ject may, without much difficulty, be determined from   regeneratio
  confifteth
  reformatio
  of manner

our *doctrinal* propofitions. Tne *firft* queftion upon this fubject is, Whether regeneration confifteth in a reformation of *manners* ? The rank Pelagians, as they deny original fin, tne lofs of original righteoufnefs, and our being in a ftate of fpiritual death ; and hold only to *external* grace, which prefcribes to man his duty, and *excites* by arguments to the performance of it : So they allow no regeneration, but what confifteth in a reformation of manners, effected by the *external* grace of God. The Socinians, thofe rankeft Pelagians, tread in their fteps, and affirm the fame with them. The Reformed confider a reformation of manners, as belonging, not to regeneration, in its ftrict and proper fenfe, but to converfion and fanctification ; while they place regeneration folely in the reformation of the inner man, the underftanding, will, and other faculties, as we have fhewn under the *doctrinal* part. Which they fupport by the following reafons, (1) Man, by breaking the covenant of works, hath loft his *original* righteoufnefs, in which the *fpiritual* life of the foul confifteth, (and by the help of which alone our firft parents were enabled to perform *fpiritual* good, as we have confidered in a former difcourfe,) and fo by fin hath contracted *fpiritual death.* (2) The fcriptures exprefly extend regeneration, to the renewing of the inner parts of the foul, to a *new heart,* a new fpirit, to the *writing* of the law upon the mind, and upon the heart ; as in the *doctrinal* part. (3) A real reformation of *manners,* cannot refult from any thing, but a previous *principle of life,* and a renewing of the mind and heart.[*] Nor have our adverfaries any thing to urge in fupport of the contrary, but their own inconfiftent fuppofitions, fuch as, (1) That the image of God did not contain *original* righteoufnefs, which we have confuted in a former difcourfe. (2) That man was not deprived of the image of God, fo far as it confifted in *original righteoufnefs,* for tranfgreffing the

law

2 Cor. 3 5 6.
1 Cor. 2 14
Rom 8 7.

Reafons of our opponents.

law of paradife. Which we have already confuted. (3) That man did not by the lofs he fuftained, contract fpiritual death and univerfal impotence to fpiritual and faving good, (which hath been already confuted.) And therefore, (4) That there is nothing needs reformation in man but his *manners* or moral conduct. The falfity of which naturally appears from what hath been already obferved.

XXIV. Queft. *Second.* Doth regeneration flow from the free will of man, or from God alone ? The rank Pelagians, with whom the Socinians exactly agree, as they fuppofe that the nature and free will of man were not impaired by the firft fin, fo they afcribe their regeneration, which they make to confift in a reformation of manners, to free will alone, excepting that they allow grace *externally* directing and influencing in a way of *moral* fuafion ; yet fuch grace as may be *rejected* by the free will of man. The Semi-Pelagians, with whom the Jefuits and Arminians agree, admit indeed, that the human nature was impaired by fin ; that *blindnefs* was thereby brought upon the underftanding, and a certain *debility (tepor)* upon the will : Therefore they hold to fome kind of *internal* grace, which may be excited, even as to the will by *external* grace in a way of moral fuafion ; but fuch as may neverthelefs be *rejected* by the free will of man. The Synergiftæ, among the Lutherans, with whom Macrelius, in his ecclefiaftical hiftory, reckons Victorinus Strigelius ; hold that the *power*, which man *naturally* hath, may contribute *fomething* towards their regeneration. The Lutherans in general hold, that a man can, by the power of his *free will*, at leaft refrain from pofitively *refifting* the Holy Spirit in the work of regeneration, i. e. by the ufe of external means, he may as it were open the door to the fpirit, when he is about to introduce the fpiritual life. The Reformed, altho' they allow, that after a fpiritual quickening is

Q 2 Whether regeneration depends upon the free-will of man ?

Different fentiments.

E effected

effected by regeneration, a man may, in conversion, co-operate with God unto the exercising of faith and repentance. Yet, in regeneration strictly so called, they deny that a man can do any thing *actively* ; but affirm that he is *merely passive.* Because, (1) *Before* regeneration is effected, man is spiritually *dead* : therefore cannot, either in whole, or in part, contribute any thing towards begetting life in himself : for this contributing of something would suppose *life.* Because, (2) In regeneration there is bestowed a new *heart*, a new *spirit*, on which is written the law of God ; which certainly is to be ascribed to God alone. (3) There is in regeneration a *creation*, and a new *creature*, which can be attributed only to God. (4) *Of ourselves* we are insufficient to think even the least thought, with which *salvation* is connected. (5) *God* is said to work in us, *to will* according to his good pleasure. (6) The scriptures expresly declare, that it is not of him that *willeth*, or of him that *runneth* ; but of God that sheweth mercy. (7) If man were, either in whole, or in part, the author of his own regeneration ; he would make himself to *differ*, contrary to the apostles assertion. Nor doth what our adversaries allege, favour their opinion in the least ; as, (1) That we are sometimes commanded to *circumcise the foreskin* of our *hearts*, to *make to ourselves a new heart, and a new spirit*, to be *renewed in the spirit of our minds*, and to *turn ourselves to God.* To this I answer, (1) It is no ways inconsistent, that God should both *command* and *freely bestow* the same thing, according to the well known expression of Austin ; *da, quod jubes* (freely give what thou commandest)—thus God commandeth love ; yet it is *he*, that shedeth it abroad in our hearts. (2) Those places of scripture, which are alleged, speak not of *regeneration*, strictly so called, by which God *infuseth* the first principle of life ; but of *conversion*, wherein he bringeth forth the life, already bestowed, into ac-

tua

tual exercise.[1] They object, (2) That if a man doth nothing towards his own regeneration, but is purely paffive, he is regenerated as a *flock*, or ftone. To which I anfwer, this by no means follows, fince the fubject of regeneration hath been previoufly taught by the *external call* of the gofpel, and by *moral* fuafion. They object, 3. That to fuppofe a perfon doth not exercife a free felf-determining power as to his regeneration, would deftroy the freedom of the will. To which I anfwer, (1) A mans free will is no more concerned in his fpiritual *regeneration*, than in his natural *generation*. (2) Regeneration is not an *action* of the man, that it fhould be determined by his free will; but a mere *paffion*, in which he only admits (or is the object of) the action of God, being capable (as a rational creature) of having fuch an action performed upon him.

[1] Cant. 1. 4.
Jer. 31. 18.
John 6. 44.
65.

XXV. Queft. *Third* Is the action of God, which regenerateth a man, *moral*, or *phyfical*? The rank Pelagians with the Socinians, as they place the nature of free will in *indifference*, and fuppofe alfo that the free will of man is unimpaired by fin, and therefore that a man, by his own *power*, can do whatfoever God requireth of him; allow nothing, but a moral *action* or agency of God in regeneration, in which, he *teacheth* what is to be done, and by motives perfuadeth to the doing of it. The Semi-Pelagians, together with the Jefuits and Arminians, as they acknowledge fome *internal* depravity as the effect of fin; fo they likewife allow fome *phyfical* agency of God in regeneration, which removes that depravity: But, as they reftrain the depravity, arifing from fin, to the *inferior* faculties of the foul, or at moft, to the underftanding; fo they allow the phyfical agency of God, only with refpect to thefe faculties: while, as to the *will* or free will of man, they hold only to a *moral* agency; yea, they fuppofe, that this *phyfical* action of God may be rejected

Q 3 whether the action of God, which regenerates, be moral or phyfical.

Different fentiments.

jected

jected by the power of the will. The Reformed, altho'
they acknowledge a moral agency of God in the *external call* of the gospel, which is previous to regeneration, and tho' they allow both a *physical* and *moral*
agency together in *conversion*, which follows regeneration. Yet in regeneration strictly so called, they admit
only a mere absolute *physical* agency. Because, (1)
Regeneration is the *first* implantation of the spiritual
life before which, the person regenerated was spiritually *dead.* Now moral *suasion* is no more sufficient,
or even conducive, to the begeting of the *spiritual,*
than it is, of the *natural* life. Because, (2) That spiritual *circumcision*—*new creation*—*taking away the heart
of stone—putting within us a heart of flesh—writing the
law thereupon*—*and drawing,* by which terms regeneration is expressed, is not a *moral,* but a purely *physical*
operation. Because, (3) *That superabundant greatness
of divine power,* which was exerted in the *raising* of
Christ from the dead, was not *moral,* but *physical* in the
highest sense And the apostle testifies, that the same
power is exerted in our regeneration.   The principal
things, which can be urged upon the contrary side,
are. (1) That we read of God's bringing about regeneration by commanding it, (which, without doubt
speaks a *moral* way of operation) as "*circumcise the
foreskin of your hearts,* make to yourselves a new heart,
work out your own salvation.*" To which I answer. In
these commands God speaks to his *church,* to his people, who had long been his *delight,* therefore they
must have been already *regenerate* ; since, without regeneration. no one can see, or *enter into* the kingdom
of God. Therefore, by these *commands,* God doth
not mean to bring about *regeneration,* as it denotes the
first infusion of the spiritual life, but the drawing
forth of that life, which is infused by regeneration
into the *second* acts or consequent exercises, (which
express*ly* mentioned in the passage,* from whence the
fir

firſt of theſe commands is quoted,) which is done in *converſion*, that follows upon regeneration, in which man *being drawn runs after God ,* being turned, he actively converts and turns himſelf to God by the power of his grace.[x]   It is objected, (2) If regeneration is effected by the *phyſical* agency of God alone, without any co operation of the man, then man is regenerated as a *ſtock* or a ſtone.   To which I anſwer, 1. Regeneration accoiding to the ſcriptures, reſpects man as ſpiritually *dead*,[a] as poſſeſſed of a *heart of ſtone*,[b] *unfit* for any *ſpiritual* exerciſes .[c] But is a man, that is ſpiritually dead, having an heart of ſtone, and being unqualified for vital operations, in any proper ſenſe, the ſame as a ſtock or a ſtone ? 2. Regeneration is wrought in man, after he hath been externally *called*, to whom grace hath been offered in a way of *moral* ſuaſion, and he invited to the reception of it ; thus, ſo far at leaſt, he is regenerated, not as a ſtock or a ſtone, but as a man: It is objected, 3 That, by a *phyſical* regeneration, the liberty of the will would be impaired and even deſtroyed.   To which I anſwer: Since by regeneration ſpiritual life is beſtowed upon the will of man, which was before dead, it is ſo far from being *deſtroyed*, that it is reſtored to its proper life and perfection.

XXVI. Queſt. *Fourth.* Doth the phyſical operation of regeneration affect the *will immediately ?* The rank Pelagians, with the Socinians, allow no phyſical operation of God at all in regeneration ; but hold only to a moral and external operation.   The Semi Pelagians, with the Jeſuits and Arminians, allow *ſome* phyſical efficiency in regeneration ; but ſuch as affects not the *will*, or free will ; but only the *other* faculties of the ſoul.   Some of the Reformed, v. g. John Cameron, and many others allow indeed a phyſical operation upon the *will* ; but that only by the *medium* of the underſtanding, which God, in regeneration, ſo
.*powerfully*

[w] Cant 1. 4

[x] Jer. 31. 18.

[a] Eph. 2. 5
[b] Ezek. 36.
25, 26, 27
[c] 2 Cor. 3. 5

Q 4. Whether the phyſical operation of regeneration affects the will immediately.

powerfully enlightens, and convinces, that the will cannot but follow it's laft practical dictate. The fynod of Dort, with moft of the Reformed, extend the phyfical operation of regeneration to the will, and that *immediately*, as it begets in the will a new *propenfity* towards fpiritual good, which, in my judgment, is moft agreeable to truth. Becaufe, (1) The fcriptures do, in exprefs terms, afcribe the phyfical agency of regeneration to the *will*,[d] *it is God that worketh in us both to will*, &c. Becaufe, (2) In terms of the fame meaning, the fcriptures extend it to the *heart*, by which is always meant the will in fcripture :[e] That God *creates* a new *heart*, and taking away the heart of ftone, *puts* this new heart within us, and *writes* his law upon it : moft certainly this is done by a *phyfical* operation. (3) The *will* is itfelf depraved by fin, as well as the underftanding, and inferior faculties ;[f] hence we frequently read of a *hard heart*, by reafon of which, man is not *fubject* to the law of God, neither indeed *can he be*.[g] (4) That corruption, which is feated in the *will*, would not be taken away by an illumination of the underftanding : nor doth the will follow the laft dictate of the practical underftanding, unlefs it dictates agreeably to the *propenfity* of the will : v. g. if the will hath a propenfity to *carnal* things, and the underftanding fhould judge, in the fulleft manner, that fpiritual things at this very time, all circumftances confidered, were to be preferred ; yet the will would not follow : becaufe the will accounts that only as *good*, which is *agreeable* to its propenfity. Nor have they, who are of the contrary opinion, any thing to object here, except, (1) That upon this fuppofition the *freedom* of the will would be taken away. Which objection we have removed in folving the preceding queftion. (2) That the will *always* follows the *laft* dictate of the practical underftanding , therefore, were the underftanding but powerfully enlightened, fo as to judge that fpiritual

things

Margin notes:

Reafons for the affirmative

Phil 2. 13

Pfal 51. 12

Ezek 36. 25
36 27

Gen 6 5.
& 8 21
Rom. 8 7.

Objections in favour of the negative

things were better *for them,* than any senfual enjoyments; the will muſt neceſſarily follow: And therefore an immediate operation of God upon the will ſeems unneceſſary, were the underſtanding but ſufficiently enlightened. To which I anſwer, (1) That laſt *actual* dictate of the practical *underſtanding* doth not take away that *habitual* corruption, which is in the *will.* (2) That, upon the whole, is *good* to the will, which is agreeable to its *inclination*; wherefore, if the practical judgment determine agreeably to this inclination of the will, the will always follows; but if contrary thereto, however powerful the dictates of the underſtanding may be; yet the will doth not obey: It is therefore neceſſary, that in regeneration, a new *propenſity* be infuſed into the will towards *ſpiritual* good, that the practical underſtanding may dictate agreeably thereto. *

XXVII.

* Preſident Edwards in his enquiry into the freedom of the will, page 12. Boſton edition, obſerves thus, with regard to the will's always following the laſt dictate of the underſtanding.

"It appears from theſe things, that in ſome ſenſe, *the will always follows the laſt dictate of the underſtanding.* But then the underſtanding muſt be taken in a large ſenſe, as including the whole faculty of perception or apprehenſion, and not merely what is called *reaſon* or *judgement.* If by the dictate of the underſtanding is meant what reaſon declares to be beſt or moſt for the perſon's happineſs, taking in the whole of his duration, it is not true that the will always follows the laſt dictate of the underſtanding. Such a dictate of reaſon is quite a different matter from things appearing now moſt agreeable, all things being put together, which pertain to the minds preſent perceptions, apprehenſions or ideas, in any reſpect Altho' that dictate of reaſon, when it takes place, is one thing that is put into the ſcales, and is to be conſidered as a thing that has concern in the compound influence which moves and induces the will; and is one thing that is to be conſidered in eſtimating the degree of that appearance of good which the will always follows, either as having its influence added to other things, or ſubducted from them When it concurs with other things, then it's weight is added to them, as put into the ſame ſcale; but when it is againſt them, it is as a weight in the oppoſite ſcale, where it reſiſts the influence of other things: yet it's reſiſtance is often overcome by their greater weight, and ſo the act of the will is determined in oppoſition to it."

Q 5. Whether regeneration be irreftible or not

Different fentiments.

XXVII. Queſt. *Fifth.* Is regeneratiou irreſiſtible or not? The rank Pelagians and Socinians, as they allow only a *moral* operation of God in regeneration, and ſuppoſe the free will of man to be equally *indifferent*, either to receive, or to reject the divine influence, ho'd it to be *reſiſtible*: The Semi-Pelagians, with the Jeſuits and Arminians, as they hold the regenerating operation to be *phyſical* in part, as it reſpects the underſtanding and interior faculties; and only *moral* in part, as it reſpects the will; they maintain that it is in the *power* of the free will, ſo to reſiſt the divine operation, that regeneration would by no means be effected. Some among the Reformed do not like the term *irreſiſtible*, tho' they admit the term *inſuperable*. We have allowed, in the *doctrinal* part, that the *moral* ſuaſion of the *external* call, and alſo converſion, ſo far as it is effected by *moral* ſuaſion, is *reſiſtible*: But re-

Arguments of the ortho·dox

James 1 18.
Rom 9 19
Phil 2 13
John10 29
Joan 6 44
6 5.

Eph. 1. 19.
20.

John 6 37·
with v 44.
Ezek. 11.
19. & 36 25,
26, 27.

John 1. 13·
Eph 2 5·

John 11.43
44.

generation we affirm o be abſolutely *irreſiſtible*; for the following reaſons. (1) Regeneration is effected by the *will* of God, which the apoſtle Paul expreſly aſſerts to be *irreſiſtible*. (2) God worketh in us both to *will* and to do, and therein taketh away all *inclination to reſiſt*. (3) By regeneration, the Father, who is *greater than all*, *draweth* thoſe who are regenerated. And, (4) Draweth them *by the ſame exceeding greatneſs of power, by which he raiſed Jeſus from the dead*. (5) He ſo *draweth* in regeneration, that they, who are drawn, do infallibly *come*. (6) By regeneration he taketh away the heart of *ſtone*, by which we make reſiſtance to the divine call. (7) God begetteth us by regeneration, which act a man can no more reſiſt, than he could his own *natural* generation. (8) By regeneration God *quickeneth*, or maketh alive, which the ſubject of regeneration can no more reſiſt, than a dead man can reſiſt his being raiſed to a *natural* life. v g. no more than Lazarus could reſiſt Chriſt. (9) If a man could reſiſt, by reaſon of the *total* corruption of his

nature,

nature,* he would continually do it.* (10) If he could *R'om. 7. 19
resist, and yet did not actually resist ; he would have and 8, 7. Isa.
of himself, the glory of not resisting, and of his own 1. 5, 6.
regeneration ; and so would make *himself* to differ, con- t Acts 7. 51.
trary to the apostle Paul's assertion." (11) If any one * 1 Cor. 4. 7.
could at his pleasure *resist* the divine agency in regeneration, then *all* could, and so it might be the case,
that not one would be regenerated, and thus the whole
glorious design of redemption might be *frustrated,*
contrary to the apostle Paul's assertion,v and the gol- v 2 Tim 2. 19.
den chain of predestination be broken.x What our x Rom. 8. 30.
adversaries object here is of no weight at all, v. g. (1) Objections
They allege the words of Stephen, *Ye always resist the* of the hete-
*Holy Ghost.*a To which I answer : They resisted the a Acts 7. 51.
Holy Ghost, not , when regenerating, but *externally*
calling, and that not indeed immediately ; but by men,
in a *moral* way, as plainly appears from the following
verse, Whom of the prophets have not your fathers persecu-
ted ? 2. They allege these words of our Saviour,
How often would I have gathered thy children together, &c.
*and ye would not ?*b To which I answer : By the ex- b Math. 23 37.
pression, *I would have gathered you,* our Saviour doth
not mean, by the exertion of a *regenerating* power, but
by calling them in a way of *moral* suasion, as the *pro-*
phets did, who were *sent* unto them for *this purpose,*
whom they stoned. 3. They object these words from
the Psalms, *O that my people had hearkened unto me, and*
*Israel had walked in my ways.*c To which I answer : c Ps. 81. 14.
The text plainly speaks of resistance made not to regeneration ; but to the *external call :* as appears
from v. 9 to 12. They object, 4. What is said in
Isaiah, *What could I have done more to my vineyard, that*
*I have not done in it ?*d To which I answer: The prophet d Isa. 5. 4.
is speaking, (1) of the benefits purchased by Christ
for the *church* in general, not of that special benefit,
which is purchased for *each* of the elect in particular.
(2) He is speaking of *external* means, not of the grace

F   of

of *regeneration* which is *internal*. They object, 5. That, upon this supposition, no one *can* be regenerated, but those who actually are so. To which I answer: With respect to *man*, it is true, no one *can* be regenerated, but he who actually is so; because all are dead in sin: but, with respect to *God*, all things are possible.[*] They object, **6.** That upon this scheme, they who resist do the *will* of God. To which I answer: They resist the *preceptive* will of God, which only prescribes to rational creatures their duty; but they do not resist the *decretive* will of God, which governs the event.

[*] Mat. 19 26.

Q 6. Whether there be any preparation to regeneration.

XXVIII. Quest. *Sixth.* Doth regeneration admit of any *preparation?* The Pelagians and Semi-Pelagians, with all their followers, the Socinians, Jesuits and Arminians, maintain the affirmative; because they hold that the efficacy of converting grace depends upon the *free will* of man; and suppose that *one* is by *nature* more prepared for converting grace than *another*; or that he can thus prepare himself by his own power. The Reformed admit indeed of preparations in regeneration, taken in a large sense, to signify the same as conversion; thus Perkins in his Cases of Conscience, Sect. I. Ch. v. vi. xi. Dr. Ames in his Caf. Con. Lib. II. Ch. iv. How far preparations may be admitted, and how far not, we have explained in the *doctrinal* part, § XIX. viz. That regeneration, understood to signify only the *first* implantation of the spiritual life, admits of no preparations, excepting what ariseth from the offers and moral invitations of the *external call* of the gospel; if you chuse to call that a preparation; because the first implantation of the spiritual life is effected in a moment, just as a resurrection to a natural life is; nor can there be any middle state between spiritual life and spiritual death.

Q 7 Whether regeneration can be ever wholly lost.

XXIX. Quest. *Seventh.* Can regeneration once wrought ever be *wholly lost?* The Pelagians, with all

the

the favourers of Pelagianiſm, maintain the affirmative;
becauſe they ſtrenuouſly hold to ſuch a *free will* in
man, as can either diveſt itſelf of grace received, or
receive it at pleaſure, (with whom, in this point at
leaſt, the Lutherans agree; as they hold that one
truly regenerate may totally fall from grace.) The
Reformed hold it can never be wholly loſt; but this
they ſuppoſe to depend, not upon the power of the *re-
generate*, but upon God's immutable decree of *election*, Reaſons of the orthodox
and his almighty upholding power: which is evident
from the following reaſons, (1) The *ſeed* of the regenerate is ſaid to abide in them.[f] (2) It is ſaid of the [f] 1 John 3.9.
regenerate, in conſequence of their being endowed
with a heart of *fleſh*, that they ſhall walk in God's ſtatutes,[g] *ſhall keep* his judgments and do them.[g] (3) It [g] Ezek. 36.
is evident from the *inſeperable* connection there is be- 26, 27.
tween predeſtination and glorification.[h] (4) The *foun-* [h] Rom. 8 30.
dation of God ſtandeth ſure, having this ſeal, The Lord
knoweth them that are his.[i] (5) The *truth* of God ſtands [i] 2 Tim. 2.19
engaged for the perſeverence of the regenerate.[k] Nor [k] 1 Pet 1. 3 4.
doth it help our adverſaries to object, (1) That a 29.
righteous man may *turn* from his righteouſneſs.[l] For [l] Ezek. 3. 20
I anſwer: The prophet is ſpeaking here, [1] of a and 18. 24.
natural power (*de potentia cauſæ*,) by which, even the the heteroʒ
truly righteous conſidered in themſelves, can fall from dox.
grace; but, not of what will actually take place (*de*
potentia effectûs) as tho' they, who are upheld by God,
could fall away into total apoſtacy. [2] The prophet
ſpeaks *conditionally*, if the righteous man ſhould turn,
he would die; and not *abſolutely*, that a truly righteous perſon can actually fall away. But, [3] The prophet doth not ſpeak of the *truly* righteous, or thoſe
who are *internally* ſo by regeneration, converſion and
ſanctification, who never can fall away;[m] but of thoſe [m] Pſ. 37.
who were righteous in *appearance* only, or in their *own* 18 20. 24.
eſtimation.[l] (2) Our adverſaries inſiſt upon there be- 125. 1. 2.
ing inſtances of thoſe who have finally fallen away; [l] Math. 9.
with Luk
as 18. 9. 10.

ʲJohn 17.12.
ᵐ2 Tim 4 10
ᵃ 1 Tim. 1.
19 20

ᵉ 1 John 3 9.

as Judas, ' Demas, ᵐ Hymeneus and Alexander :ᵃ T
which I answer, It remains to be proved that they
were ever truly regenerated; this text is expresly a-
gainst it ;ᵉ *Whosoever is born of God doth not commit fin,*
for his feed remaineth in him, and he cannot fin ; because he
is born of God. They object (3) That there are certainly instances of the truly regenerate, who have fallen from grace, in the drunkenness of Noah, the
adultery and murther of David, Peter's denying his
Lord, &c. To which I answer, They omitted, or rather neglected some *second* acts or exercises of the spiritual life ; but they never wholly lost the *first* act or

ᵖ Psal 51. 13. principle, which was bestowed in regeneration. ᵖ They
object, (4) If the regenerate *cannot* lose the grace of
regeneration, they would cease to be *free agents.* To
which I answer, The consequence by no means follows ; since the constant presence of the spiritual life
in the will rather *confirms* the liberty of it.

ɋQ 8 Whether
regeneration
be universal.

Different
sentiments:

XXX Quest. *Eighth.* Whether regeneration be *uni*
versal, or whether all men are regenerated ? *All the*
Papists, as well the Dominicans, as the Jesuits, (as
they suppose *sufficient grace* given to every man, whereby he *can be saved,* do, in effect, hold regeneration to
be *universal,* (since according to the scriptures, in regeneration properly so called, there is conferred only
a *power* to perform spiritual good, as we have shewn
under the *doctrinal* part.) However, in the explanati-
on of this sufficient grace, they greatly differ. The
Dominicans indeed suppose that *sufficient* grace is given to all ; but yet such as cannot put forth itself into
actual exercise, without *efficacious* grace preceeding.
But the Jesuits hold to sufficient grace, whose *efficacy*
depends upon the free will of every man. The rank
Pelagians and Socinians, as they make regeneration to
consist in a *reformation of manners,* suppose sinners have
by nature, that power, whereby they *can* regenerate
themselves, or reform their moral conduct : But the
d

do not fuppofe that an *actual* reformation of manners takes place in every one ; but only in thofe, who *will* to reform their moral conduct. They exprefly exclude regeneration from *infants*, both on account of their having no inherent fin, and alfo on account of their incapacity, from the want of reafon, to reform their moral conduct. Among the Reformed who hold to *univerfal* grace, there are fome who fuppofe, that by the grace of God power is *reftored* to *all*, and every man, whereby they can be faved, if they *will* ; altho' there is given to the *elect* alone that power, by which they are actually made willing. The renowned Cocceius, altho' he doth not deny that regeneration took place under the old teftament ; yet in the emphatical fenfe of it, he confines it to new teftament times. The general opinion of the Reformed is, that the grace of regeneration is in the higheft fenfe peculiar to all the *elect* ; and they fuppofe alfo that even *infants* are fometimes the fubjects of it, which they fupport by the following reafons, (1) The fcriptures, as often as they make mention of regeneration, extend it, not to *all* promifcuoufly ; but to the *elect* only,[q] and that, (2) To the *exclufion* of all others.[r] (3) The fcriptures exprefly declare, there are fome who have not this *power* which is conferred in regeneration.[s] Yea, (4) The fcriptures do extend regeneration particularly to *infants*.[t] Nor can any place of fcripture be produced by our adverfaries to the contrary, which teftifieth, either that regeneration, the fpiritual life, a power of performing fpiritual good, or fufficient grace is granted to all and *every* one.

XXXI. Queft. *Ninth*. Whether regeneration be *neceffarily connected* with baptifm ? The Socinians rightly deny it ; but upon a wrong hypothefis, that the baptifm of water is but an indifferent rite, introduced by the apoftles, without the command of Chrift, having no ufe or efficacy. The Anabaptifts likewife deny

The general opinion of the reformed with their reafons.

[q] 1 Pet. 1.
Eph. 2. 3 4. 5
James 1. 1
John 3. 3—
[r] John 6. 4
44. 64. 65
[s] Rom. 8.
Jer. 13. 2
[t] Jer. 1. 5.
Luke 1. 1
2 Tim. 3. 1

Q. 9. Whether regeneration be neceffarily connected with baptifm.

deny it, who allow no use or efficacy of baptism, but that of *signifying* the *church* covenant, and distinguishing those who are in *that covenant*, from those who are without. On the other hand, the Papists, in order to maintain that the sacraments of the new testament beget grace *ex opere operato*, or of their own proper virtue ; hold that the baptism of water effects regeneration, hence they frequently use baptism and regeneration to signify the same thing. The Lutherans do not indeed atribute any regenerating *efficacy* to the baptismal water ; however they so confine the regenerating influences of the spirit to baptism, that they suppose no one can ordinarily be regenerated without it. The Reformed, tho' they unanimously hold that there is no *physical* regenerating efficacy in baptism ; but only a *moral* efficacy, which consists in its being a *sign and seal* of regeneration ; and also that the grace of regeneration is not confined to any sacrament ; and yet that baptism is not a mere naked, useless *sign*, but a most efficacious *sealing* of the covenant of grace and of *regeneration*, to those who receive it agreeably to it's institution, and also to the *elect infants* of believers : yet as to the manner and time of it's becoming effectual they somewhat differ. Indeed as to the baptism of *adults*, that, if *rightly* administered, doth, by the consent of all the orthodox, certainly presuppose regeneration as already effected ; because it expresly requires faith of the subject of baptism, and such faith indeed as proceeds from the *whole heart* ;[a] which cannot take place without a previous regeneration : for whatsoever is born of the flesh, is flesh ; and whatsoever is born of the spirit is spirit.[b] But as to the baptism of *infants*, here the orthodox are divided ; some deny that regeneration can *precede* baptism, which therefore, as they suppose, only seals regeneration as *future*, when the elect infant shall arrive to years of discretion, so as to be capable of faith and repentance ; thus

[a] Acts 8. 36, 37

[b] John 3. 6.

thus the celebrated Amyraldus. But he inaccurately confounds *regeneration*, which beſtows the ſpiritual life in the *firſt* act or principle, (by which the infant is effectually enabled, when he arrives to the exerciſe of reaſon, to believe and repent,) with *converſion* ; which includes the *actual* exerciſes of faith and repentance ; which cannot take place before the years of diſcretion. Others, from modeſty declining to determine the point, think it depends on the ſovereign will of God, whether to beſtow regeneration *before* baptiſm, at the time of its adminiſtration, or afterwards ; thus Zanchy in hisCommen. upon Eph. v. in a digreſſion concerning baptiſm ; and Ames in his Bellarminus enervatus Tom III. XIV. Queſt. III. Spanheim the father in his Dub. Evang. Part III. Dub. XXVII. Others chuſe to think that regeneration is effected at the *very time* of baptiſm, *ordinarily* at leaſt : Thus Lewis Le Blanc, with the Papiſts and Lutherans, who ſuppoſe this always to be the caſe, thus the celebrated Peter Jurieu, Beza, and others. The common opinion of the Reformed is, that the baptiſm of infants (at leaſt of the *elect*) preſuppoſes regeneration as already effected ; becauſe that which is not, cannot be *ſealed* by baptiſm. And this opinion appears to me moſt agreeable to truth. Before baptiſm itſelf doth not *effect* regeneration, as the Papiſts ſuppoſe ; Nor are the regenerating influences of the Holy Spirit *confined* to external baptiſm, as the Lutherans would have it. Becauſe, (1) The *efficacy* of baptiſm conſiſts in it's *ſealing*, agreeably to the nature of all ſacraments ſo far as they are *ſeals* ;[c] which preſuppoſes regeneration, as the principle of faith. Becauſe, (2) The pollution of the ſoul is not purged away by the baptiſm of water,[d] therefore regeneration is not confined thereto. And, (3) If this was the caſe, all the baptized would be regenerate, and that, at the very time of their baptiſm : Againſt which the ſcriptures ſpeak,[e] and alſo experience ſhews, that

The general opinion of the reformed, with their reaſons,

[c] Rom. 4. 11

[d] 1 Pet. 3. 21

[e] Acts 8. 13, 20, 21. 23,

that many baptized perfons live moft abandoned lives, and are not finally faved. We read alfo of perfons regenerated *before* their baptifm, as the Eunuch,[f] the Centurion and his family ;[g] yea, of thofe who were *never* baptized at all, as the thief upon the crofs ;[h] according to the common obfervation, *that it is not the want of baptifm, but the contempt of it that is damning.* (4) Regeneration is limited to no facrament, not to *circumcifion,*[i] not to the *paffover,*[k] not to the *Lord's fupper,*[k] nor to any legal wafhings,[l] therefore not to baptifm, fince 'tis exprefly faid, that even a baptized perfon, if he believes not, fhall be damned.[m] I will only add, (5) That the Holy Ghoft is faid to regenerate according to his fovereign pleafure ; *as the wind bloweth where it lifteth, fo is every one born of the Spirit.*[n] 'Tis however alleged in favour of the contrary fide, (1) That Chrift hath infeparably connected regeneration with *water and the fpirit.*[o] To which I anfwer : He doth not mean the external water of baptifm, which at that time was not inftituted as an ordinary and univerfal facrament of the new-teftament ; but by an *Hendiadis,* he means the water of the Spirit, or the Spirit cleanfing, like water, in the work of regeneration. In like manner it is faid, *he will baptize you with the Holy Ghoft and with fire,*[p] i. e. with the Spirit, having the purifying quality of fire ; which our Saviour fufficiently fhews to be his meaning, when he afcribes regeneration to the Spirit alone :[q] Compare herewith what hath been faid upon this point in the *explanatory* part. 'Tis alleged, (2) That the wafhing away of fin,[q] regeneration,[r] and falvation[s] are afcribed to baptifm ; therefore baptifm either works regeneration by it's own virtue, or at leaft the Holy Spirit hath infeparably connected his regenerating influences therewith. To which I anfwer : Neither of thefe is the cafe ; but only that the Holy Spirit, by baptifm, fealeth regeneration to the elect ; as we have already, obferved.

[f] Acts 8. 36. 37.
[g] Acts 10 2 22. [h] Luke 23
[i] Rom. 2. 25 27, 28
[a] 1 Cor 10 3 4 [k] 1 Cor. 11 27 [l] Heb 9. 10 & ch 10 4
[m] Mark 6 16.
[n] J hn 3. 8.
Objections.
[o] John 3. 3 5.
[p] Mat. 3. 11.
[q] John 3.6 8.
[q] Acts 22 16.
[r] Tit 3. 5.
[s] 1 Pet. 3. 21.

obferved. (3) They argue on the other fide from this text, *Know ye not, that fo many of us as were baptized into Jefus Chrift, were baptized into his death?* To which I anfwer : This text means only that all the elect, being true believers, baptized according to inftitution, have communion and participation in the death of Chrift, which is fealed to them by baptifm : But it is not faid that this communion is effected particularly by baptifm, much lefs, that this communion is abfolutely connected with baptifm. 'Tis argued, (4) As many as are baptized into Chrift, *put on Chrift*, confequently are regenerated ° To which I anfwer : The text doth not fay that they *put on* Chrift by baptifm ; but that they, who are baptized, had *before* put on Chrift. Since therefore communion with Chrift, which is fignified by the term of putting on Chrift, hath been already effected in baptized perfons, 'tis not effected by baptifm ; but being already effected, is fealed by this facrament. (5) 'Tis argued by thofe of the contrary opinion, that theirs is the received opinion of the fathers, and alfo of eminent men among the Reformed themfelves, v. g. of Auftin and Profper among the Fathers, of Pareus, Davenant, Ward and Forbes among the Reformed. To which I anfwer : The Fathers, whenever they fpeak of baptifm, are wont to ufe very ftrong expreffions ; neverthelefs, they very often fuppofe regeneration and faith as previous to baptifm : Thus Juftin Martyr, reprefenting the practice of the primitive church, faith, *"Whoever have been perfuaded and have believed—and have received power fo to live—are then brought by us to the water and are* REGENERATED, *after the fame mode of regeneration, in which we ourfelves have been regenerated."* The Fathers therefore can by no means be reconciled with each other, without a diftinction of regeneration into *real*, which *precedes* baptifm, and *facramental* which confifts in a folemn profeffion, declaration and fealing of that,

Rom. 6. 3.

Gal. 3. 27.

which,

which is *real.* In which fenfe the Reformed divines alfo hold that regeneration is effected by baptifm.

THE PRACTICAL PART.

XXXII You will now perhaps, reader, promife yourfelf a very large application of this important fubject, fince practical writers have fo much exerted themfelves upon it. But, if I fhall not fully anfwer your expectations, you will confider thefe two things. (1) Thofe practical writers treat the fubject of regeneration in a *larger* fenfe, as comprehending the *whole* internal operation of the Holy Spirit upon the redeemed, in which are contained vocation, fpiritual quickening, converfion and fanctification ; whilft we have taken it in a *ftricter* fenfe, as denoting only the beftowment of the *firft act* or principle of fpiritual life : Hence they bring under regeneration thofe things which properly belong to converfion and fanctification. If the reader is pleafed to confider this fubject in the fame latitude with them ; he may, without much difficulty, apply here, what is faid, by way of improvement, under the heads of converfion and fanctification. (2) It is to be confidered here, that the *firft* act of life is conferred, only in order to the *fecond* acts, as habits are only in order to their fecond acts or exercifes ; nor can it be known or difcerned, but by the exercifes of it : and alfo that an unregenerate perfon cannot ftrive to beget life in himfelf, or cannot difpofe himfelf thereto, fince he is merely *paffive* in the reception of the fpiritual life : Wherefore you will not wonder, if we do not labour fo much upon the practical part of this fubject. However the fubject of regeneration teacheth us,

XXXIII. *Firft.* How great a work it is to recover the finner to life ; fo that reafon, not without caufe, enquires with Nicodemus, *How can a man be born again when he is old ?* And juftly were the apoftles aftonifhed, upon a fimilar topic, when they cried out, *Who*

then

ken can be faved ?[x] For if you confider the fubject, who is to be made alive ; he is fpiritually *dead*, dead in fin ;[a] *who feeing doth not fee, and bearing doth not bear, or underftand.*[b] If you confider the *work itfelf,*[c] this is effected only by a fecond *generation,*[c] *a creation,*[d] *quickening,*[e] *taking away the heart of ftone, putting within us a heart of flefh, writing the law of God upon the heart,*[f] *or by a renovation of the whole man.*[g] If you confider the *manner* of operation, this requireth in the author of it, (1) *Infinite power, a fuperabundant greatnefs of power,*[h] as great, and, if poffible, even greater, than was exercifed in creation : Becaufe there was not only no neceffity, in order to creation, of the *death* of the Son of God, as there is in the reftoring of a finner to life : But there was no *contrary* difpofition of the object, fuch as an heart of ftone, which knows not how to beleve, fuperable by nothing fhort of *infinite* ftrength : As great a power alfo is neceffary, as was required to raife the dead.[i] (2) It requires in the author of regeneration, infinite or exhauftlefs *goodnefs* and mercy,[k] by which, that we may not all *perifh* eternally by the firft generation, he is pleafed to add a *fecond :* And left, by the *firft* life, we contract eternal death, he is pleafed to add the *fecond :* And that our fouls may not be dead in *living* bodies, he is pleafed to reftore to them the *fpiritual* life loft by fin. It requires, (3) Infinite, or the moft abfolute *fovereignty ;*[l] hereby, paffing by whom he will, he beftows the fpiritual life on whom he *pleafes :* paffing by for the moft part, the more noble, and as it were the more *worthy,* he beftows it on the more *mean* and contemptible,[m] and of materials in themfelves fo *unfuitable,* he is pleafed to rear an edifice fo *magnificent.* As appears in the cafe of Zacheus[n] —of Paul[o]—of the harlots in preference to the reputable Pharifees.[p] Regeneration inculcates the greatnefs of the work of reftoring a finner to *life,* for thefe ends, (1) That we might more particularly acknow-

[x] Mat. 19. 25
[a] Eph. 2. 1. 5
[b] Mat. 13. 13. 14. 15.
[c] John 3. 3. 5
[d] Pfalm 51. 12. Eph. 2. 10
[e] Eph. 2. 5 6.
[f] Ezek 36. 25, 26
[g] 2 Cor. 5 17.
[h] Eph. 1. 19 20

[i] Eph. 1 20.
[k] Eph 2. 4 5. and ch. 3 8. 9.

[l] Rom 9. 15. 16. 18.

[m] 1 Cor 1. 25. —29
[n] Luke 19 2. 5 8.
[o] 1 Tim. 1. 13 14
[p] Mat. 21 31.

ledge, what great *obligations* we are under to God, that
he hath regenerated and brought us into a ftate of life,
while fo many thoufands are paffed by, and that we
might fhew ourfelves more ready to make *grateful* re-

ᵃ 1 Tim.1.13. turns.ᵃ (2) That, on account of the infinite power,
goodnefs and benevolence, which God hath exhibited
in our regeneration, we might be the more careful to

ᶻ 1 P.t 1. 3. live to his glory ᶻ (3) That with regard to our future
happnefs, we might more humbly depend upon his
grace, and work out our falvation with *fear and trembling* ; becaufe it is *God* alone, who worketh in us both

ᵉ Ph'l. 2. 13 *to will ard to do.*ᵉ (4) That we might not, from our
ftate's being better than that of others, *exalt* ourfelves

ᵗ Luke 18 11. above them ;ᵗ that we might not *boaft*,ᵘ fince it is God

ᵘ Eph 2 5 alone, who, by regeneration, makes us to differ from
the worft of mankind ; and whatever good we have

ʷ 1 Cor.4 7. above them, we derive it wholly from him.ʷ (5
That we might not wonder if the moft powerful ar
guments to converfion, ufed by men, have not alway
anfwerable fuccefs ; fince it is not *of Paul, that plant
eth, nor Apollos, that watereth, but of God, that giveth th*

ˣ 1 Cor. 3 6 7 *increafe* ;ˣ for the Spirt in his regenerating influence

ᶻ Tohn 3. 8 *bloweth where he lifteth,*ᶻ and the *natural* man is natu

ᵇ Eph.2 1.5. rally *dead in fin* ;ᵇ and the Father *draweth* not all pro

ᶜ John 6. 44
64 65. mifcuouf,.ᶜ (6) That we might not readily defpa
of the converfion of *any one*, however great his opp

ᶜ 2 Tim 2..25.
26. fition thereto may be,ᶜ for the Spirit is *able* to reg
nerate and quicken him, when it feemeth good in h
fight

2. It recom
mends to us
the b'effed-
nefs of the
regenerate
ᵉ 1 Pet. 1. 3.
ᶠ John 1 13.
ᵍ Luke15 32
ʰ Ep 2.10 Pf.
100 3 com-
pared wth XXXIV. *Secondly* This fubject recommends to
the *happy* condition of thofe, who, with fo much d
ficulty have been brought, by egeneration, to a fp
ritual life : *Bleffed be God—who hath begotten us to a liv
hope* ᵉ—For, (1) *they are born not of flefh, nor of the
of man, but of God* ᶠ (2) They are made *alive* from
dead ᵍ (3) They are by way of eminence the *wo
menfhip* of God ;ʰ in a peculiar manner produced
hi

him [i] (4) They are *new creatures*,[k] in many respects [1] Tit. 2. 14.
more excellent than any other creature. For whilst [k] 2 Cor 5 17.
every other creature flows from the *common* goodness [1] Psa 104.31.
of the Creator ;[l] this *new* creature flows from his *sin-* and 145 9.
gular grace and promise [m] Whilst every other creature [m] Eph 2 4 5.
performs the work of *common* providence ;[n] this *new* [n] Acts 17 25.
creature performs the work of gracious predestination.[o] 28
Whilst every other rejoices, only in the *natural* bene- [o] Rom 8 29
fits of God ; this new creature is loaded with *spiritual* 30. Jam. 1 18.
blessings [p] (5) Instead of an insensible, *stoney* heart, [p] Pf. 4 7. 8 &
they have a heart of *flesh*, easily affected, which carries 17 14 15
the law of God written upon it.[q] (6) From persons Eph 2 4 5 6
dead, they are become spiritually *alive.*[r] (7) They [q] Ezek. 35
carry about them the Divine Image, which is restored 25. 26
to them, which is their peculiar prerogative, h. e. *ori-* [r] Eph. 2. 4 5.
ginal righteousness.[s] And what is more, (8) They are [s] Eph 4. 2
made partakers of a *divine nature.*[t] Yea, by regene- 24. Col 3 1
ration, since they are *born of God,*[u] they become the [t] 2 Pet 1
children of God ; not only by adoption, or *declaration,* [u] John 1.
as Jacob the patriarch adopted Ephraim and Manaf- & 1 Joh. 5.1
feth ;[w] but also by a spiritual *generation.* How are the [w] Gen 48.
regenerate *enabled* hereby [x] How glorious is their *in-* [x] 1 John 3
heritance [a] How great is the *liberty* of the sons of [a] Rom 8.
God [b] How free their *access* to God in every difficul- [b] Rom 8
ty [c] How great their *security* under the paternal and [c] Rom 8.
domestic care of their heavenly Father [d] (9) They Gal. 4. 6.
are by this spiritual generation endowed with *eyes*, by [d] Eph. 2. 18
which they *can see* the kingdom of God,[e] and *spiritually* [e] John 3. 3
discern the spiritual objects of it ;[f] and moreover with [f] 1 Cor. 2.
a *heart*, by which they are both able and willing *to* 15.
enter into the kingdom of God.[g] If now you cast up [g] John 3.
the sum of all these blessings, good God ! how great
doth the *blessedness* of the truly regenerate appear to be ?
How careful then should we be to represent it aright ?
That such may *congratulate* themselves upon this unspeakable gift of God :[h] That they may be filled with [h] Pf. 116.
gratitude to God :[i] That they may *shew* to others the [i] 1 Pet.

greatness

Luke 8. 39.
Mat. 5. 16
Pet. 1 2.

It repre-
sents the mi-
sery of the
unregenerate
in six parti-
culars.

John 3 3 5.
John 1 13
John 8 42. 44
2 Tim 2 26.
Eph 2 1. 5
Ezek 37 1 2
1 Cor. 2. 14.
Acts 7. 51
Ezek 36 25
Eph 4 18 19
Jer 6. 10
Acts 7. 51.
Rom. 8. 7
compared
with 2 Cor
3.

Pf. 32 9.
Rom. 1. 31.

Mat. 22. 32.

Mark 14 21.
compared
with Job 3 3
and Jer. 20.
15
Eph. 2. 10

Mat. 25 41.
66. 24

greatnefs of this bleffing, to excite their eager defires
and longings after it [k]

XXXV. *Thirdly.* This fubject reprefents, upon the
other hand, the unfpeakable *misery* of thofe, who are
deftitute of the grace of regeneration Becaufe, (1)
They *cannot* even *see* the kingdom of God, much lefs
enter therein ; hence they are utterly excluded from
the very threfhold of eternal falvation.[l] (2) So long
as they are not born *of God,*[m] they are born of their
father the devil, and fo are the children of the devil,[n]
entangled in his *fnares.*[o] (3) They are fpiritually *dead*
in fins,[p] they *see* not the things of the fpirit [q]—have
hearts of *ftone*—are *obftinate* in wickednefs,[r] and are
immoveable to that which is good.[s] They are alfo
ftupid, infenfible,[t] *impenetrable* by any moral operations
of the Holy Spirit.[u] Yea, they are *ftriving* againft the
fpirit :[x] They are not *fubject* to the law of God, neither
indeed *can* they be.[z] So that you might fooner
fqueeze *water* from a *ftone,* than excite repentance in
them They are like ftones, *cold,* deftitute of all
warmth, of all *fpiritual* love towards God, his grace,
or the falvation of their own fouls :[a] They are without natural affection (*aftorgoi* ;)[b] and from all thefe
things, furely without the *covenant of grace* ; for God
is not a God of the *dead* [c] (4) So long as they remain
unregenerate, it were better for them not to have been
born, which our Saviour exprefly declares concerning
Judas ;[d] and the unregenerate, in hell hereafter, will
curfe the day of their *birth.* (5) So long as they are
not the *workmanfhip* of God by the grace of regeneration,[e] it were better for them never to have been *created* by God, befure not to have been made *men* ; but
rather the loweft and moft defpicable reptiles : becaufe
from the immortality of their fouls, immortal, yea,
eternal *mifery* awaits them ;[f] whilft thefe reptiles will
be forever infenfible. (6) So long as they are not, by
regeneration, brought back to God, they are *alienated*

from

from the life of God,[g] are *afar off* from God,[h] with an immense *gulph*, as it were, fixed between them.[i] They are caſt out with Cain from the *preſence* of God;[k] are *without* God in the world;[l] are afar off from the *knowledge* of God, and of divine things,[m] ſeeking after God, as it were by *feeling* after him in the dark,[n] afar off alſo from the *love* and *ſaving grace* of God;[o] and alſo from *Chriſt*, from the *commonwealth* of Iſrael, from the covenants of promiſe and from all hope of ſalvation.[p] To paint in the moſt lively manner this great miſery of the unregenerate is of great ſervice, (1) To *ourſelves*, that we may hence conceive a greater *horror* of that ſtate, and groan out with David, *Create in me a clean heart, O God. and renew a right ſpirit within me,*[q] *that we might work out our own ſalvation with fear and trembling: for it is God which worketh in us, both to will and to do:*[r] And that we might *rejoice with trembling,*[s] in that we have received the grace of regeneration. (2) It may be of ſervice to *others*, who are yet in an unregenerate ſtate, that, by divine aſſiſtance, *they might awake (or recover themſelves) from the ſnares of the devil,*[*] *by which, they are led captive at his will.*[t]

XXXVI. *Fourthly.* This ſubject admoniſhes us that we ſhould *avoid* more than we would the moſt venomous animal, the reſting, in the buſineſs of our ſouls ſalvation, in any thing, however ſpecious, ſhort of *regeneration.* And that for the following reaſons. (1) It appears from the moſt ſolemn repeated aſſertions of our Saviour, that it is impoſſible, without regeneration, either to *ſee* or *enter* into, the kingdom of God.[u] (2) Whatever *is born of the fleſh*, h. e. proceeds from a *carnal* unregenerate man, is only *carnal.*[w] (3) Thouſands, by taking things *natural* for things *ſpiritual*, nature for *grace*, a good natural diſpoſition for regeneration, have miſerably deceived themſelves, and under this deception have periſhed eternally;[x] and our

Marginal references:

[g] Eph. 4. 18.
[h] Eph. 2. 13.
[i] Luke 16. 26.
[k] Gen. 4. 14.
[l] Eph. 2. 12.
[m] Eph. 4. 18.
[l] Cor. 2. 14.
[n] Acts 17. 27.
[o] Iſa. 59. 2.

[p] Eph. 2. 12.

For what end this repreſentation is to be made.

[q] Pſ. 51. 12.

[r] Phil. 2. 13.
[s] Pſ. 2. 11.

[t] 2 Tim. 2. 26.

4. That we ſhould not reſt in any thing which is not abſolutely connected with regeneration.

[u] John 3. 3. 5.
[w] John 3. 6.

[x] Luk. 18. 11. 12.

*In our tranſlation "who are taken captive by him at his will."

ourSaviour declares that Publicans and Harlots should enter into the kingdom of God *before* the Pharisees.[a] Particularly we should avoid, in the business of our salvation, resting, (1) In a more *virtuous, natural* disposition : By which thro' a certain native *goodness of temper,* as tho' they were formed of pure clay, some among the Heathen have been more inclined than others, to mildness, humanity, civility, clemency, equity, and the like ; upon which account the more moral *Pharisee* gives thanks to God, that he was not like other men, particularly the Publican, who was standing near him.[o] Nor, (2) should we rest in any natural *gifts* which may be acquired ; wherein one excelleth another among the Gentiles, and likewise among pretended Christians. v. g. In learning, wisdom, prudence, skill in mechanicks or philosophy, v.g. such as Anithophel,[y] Bezaleel and Aholiab[d] were possessed of. Nor, (3) in *moral virtues,* from which the Gentiles are said to have the *law of God written upon their hearts,*[c] yea they are said to do, *by nature the things contained in the law,*[z] in which virtues, (v. g) Plato, Cato, Scipio, Cicero, Aristides, Seneca, and the Antonini, a thousand degrees exceeded Cataline, Caligula, Nero, Heliogabulus, and others. Yea the Gentiles have herein some times out-done God's *professing* people. v. g. Tyre and Sidon excelled the inhabitants of Bethsaida and Chorazin :[s] The Sodomites, the inhabitants of Capernaum ,[h] and the queen of the South, the Jews.[i] Nor, (4) may we rest in any *ecclesiastical* or external duties of religion ; such as the *acknowledgement* of the truth,[k] the *profession* of it,[l] *disputing* for it,[m] a frequent *attendance* upon holy exercises,[n] the use of the sacraments,[o] bestowing of alms,[p] fasting,[q] suffering martyrdom for the truth,[r] *preaching* the word,[u] or in a *zealous* profession.[x] Nor, (5) may we rest in any kind of external *righteousness,*[a] a conversation that is morally honest,[b] or a blameleisness as to their righteousness of

law,

Mat 21. 31.

In what things we should by no means rest.

Luke 18.11. 12.

2 Sam 16 23
Ex-o 31.2
Rom 2 15
ver. 14
Mat 11.21.
v 23
Mat 12 24
Rom 2 18
22. 1 Cor. 3 2.
Rom 2. 17
Mar.8 21 22
1 Cor. 1.19
o. Luke 18
1 If. 1. 15
1 Cor. 10.
3.4 Acts 8.
3 Gal. 5 6
or 11 27.
Luke 18 12.
Cor. 13 3.
Luke 18 12
1 Cor. 15.3.
Mat. 7.21 22
Cor. 13. 1
Phil 3. 6
Mat 5. 20
Luke 18 11.
2.

law.[c] Nor, (6) may we reſt in the gifts of *common* grace ;[d] ſuch as, (1) the common *illumination* of the Holy Spirit ,[e] in conſequence of which, we may acknowledge the ſaving truth, receive it with joy, profeſs it courageouſly, and preach it with zeal : (2) The powerful *reſtraining* influences of the ſpirit.[f] (3) Some kind of *deteſtation* and avoidance of enormous crimes.[g] (4) A kind of *repentance* for groſs ſins, wherein we acknowledge them, are ſorry for them, confeſs them, and in a degree reform our lives, as Judas did :[h] (5) An *external* obſervance of the law and precepts of God [i] In all theſe things therefore, and many others, a man muſt never *reſt*, in the great buſineſs of his ſalvation, if he means not to be deceived ; for all theſe things may be found in perſons deſtitute of the ſpirit, or his *regenerating* influences, ariſing merely from *fleſhly* principles, therefore they may be only of a *carnal* nature :[k] Altho' in the truly regenerate theſe things may take their origin from the ſpirit or the ſpiritual life infuſed. Wherefore it is abſolutely neceſſary, that in all theſe things, we accurately diſtinguiſh the *nature* of them from the grace of regeneration, and mark their defects. from which we may clearly know, that they flow not from the *ſpirit*, or the ſpiritual life of regeneration ; but from the *fleſh*, that is from unregenerate nature. Thoſe *moral* duties therefore differ from ſpiritual ones. 1. As to their *origin* ; for whilſt ſpiritual things originate from the *ſpirit*,[l] and are the fruit of the ſpirit,[m] and proceed from the law of God, written by the ſpirit upon the heart ;[n] thoſe moral duties are effected *merely* by induſtry, ſtudy and practice, and are excited by the powers of free will, and are therefore only the works of *nature*, not of the *ſpirit*. 2. They differ as to the *rule* : whilſt *ſpiritual* duties conform themſelves to the rule of the *new creature*,[o] and they, that are ſpiritual walk after the *ſpirit*,[p] and according to the will of God ;[q] the *morality* of the

[c] Phil. 3. 6.
[d] Heb 6 4.
[e] Num. 24 5 4

[f] Gen. 20. 6.
[g] 1 Cor 5. 1.

[h] Math. 27. 3.
4 5
1 King 21 27.
1 Mat 19.18.
19. 20.

[k] John 3. 6.

How moral duties differ from ſpiritual.
[l] John 3 5.
[m] Gal. 5. 22.
[n] Jer. 31. 33.
Ezek. 36, 26, 27.

[o] Gal 6. 16.
[p] Rom. 8. 1.
[q] Mat. 6. 10.

H   unregenerate

unregenerate is regulated by a kind of *mediocrity,* which reason and the sentiments of wise men have fixed. Therefore this morality is not obedience performed unto *God,* but to *reason* and wise men. 3. They differ as to the *end :* whilst the *regenerate,* in the performance of *spiritual* duties, aim at the *glory* of God, and after union and communion with him, in which their greatest happiness consisteth : The *unregenerate* in their *moral* duties seek chiefly their *own* glory and interest, as was evidently the case with the Pharisees : or if something higher excites them to the pursuit of *virtue,* at most 'tis only the *beauty* of virtue, as being *agreeable* to reason. 4. They differ as to the immediate *cause :* whilst spiritual duties flow from faith, which accounts as sin whatsoever is not of *itself,* however specious it may appear : These *moral* duties know nothing of *faith,* they grow from the seeds of *nature,* and are watered by exercise, without any earnest seeking of divine assistance. 5. They differ as to the *foundation :* whilst all *spiritual* duties have their existence, and are performed in *Christ,* without whom we can do nothing, and by whom we *can do all things ;* nor are they acceptable to God, except in Christ the beloved ; as, by his righteousness he covers, and makes amends for, all the defects of these duties, and so presents them to his father : The *morality* of the unregenerate hath *nothing* of Christ in it, and is therefore but the *tares of nature,* their own righteousness, and like a *menstruous* garment, abominable in the sight of God. 6. They differ as to the *affection* of humility : whilst *spiritual* exercises are joined with a constant sense and acknowledgement of their native unfitness and corruption, and consequently with profound humility : This *morality puffeth up* and savours rankly of pride and arrogance.

*1 Cor 10.31
Phil. 1 20
* Psf 16. 5. &
73 25.

* Mat. 6 2.5.

* Rom 1 17
Gal 2. 20
* Rom.14 23

* John 15. 5.
* Phil 4 13
* Eph. 1 6

* If 64 6.
* Luke 17 10
and 18. 13
* 2 Cor. 3 5.
* Mat.6.2 5.8.
* Luke 18. 11
* 2 If 58 2 3.
* Mat. 7. 26.

XXXVII.

XXXVII. *Fifthly.* This subject recommends to us, an impartial *examination* of ourselves, that we may know, whether we are truly regenerate or not. Altho' the *first* act or principle of spiritual life, which is conferred in regeneration, be not *evident of itself*, any more than the *first* act or principle of natural life, or any habit or virtue : It is however very conspicuous in its *operations*, which it puts forth in conversion : and altho' a person, before one of good *moral conversation*, cannot easily be certain that he is *not* regenerate, because the life of regeneration may sometimes, like seed in the earth, lie hid for a time : however he that is truly regenerated and converted can, from the *fruits* of the spirit, [d] be absolutely certain of his regeneration and conversion : [e] Before he, that brings *not* forth fruits, meet for repentance, may justly *doubt* of his regeneration, so as to be sensible that he stands in need of it. By what evidences then shall I certainly know that I am regenerated ? I answer by these which follow, 1. Whoever experiences within himself a general *renovation*, by which, from a *carnal*, worldly man, he becomes *spiritual* and heavenly, he without doubt is regenerate : for regeneration is the *renovation* of the Holy Spirit, [f] and a regenerate person is a *new creature*, [g] who hath received a *new* heart, a *new* spirit, [h] and is *transformed* into the *image of God*, [i] so that it is no longer *he that liveth*, but *Christ in him*. [k] 2. Whoever, instead of his former *blindness*, experiences new *light*, by which he can know and discover spiritual objects in a *spiritual* manner, he is most certainly regenerate. [l] 3. Whoever, in his heart and will, experiences a new *propensity* towards spiritual objects, he without doubt is a regenerate person. [m] 4. Whoever in the *affections* or passions of his soul, in love and hatred, desire and aversion, joy and sorrow ; likewise anger, fear and courage, experiences a more *spiritual* constitution than before ; he is most certainly regenerate. [n] 5. Whoever seriously strive after *growth* in spiritual things, that they may

5. This subject recommends examination of ourselves, whether we are truly regenerate or not ?

By what evidences a man may be certain that he is regenerate.

[d] Gal. 5. 22.
Mat 7 16.—
21.
[e] 1 John 5 14
and 5. 1.
[f] Tit. 3. 5
[g] 2 Cor. 5. 1
[h] Ezek 36 26
[i] 2 Cor. 3 18
[k] Gal. 2. 20
[l] Eph 1. 1
& 5 8. 1 Co
2. 14. 15.
2 Cor 4 3.
Acts 26. 1
[m] Phil 3. 7.
Psal. 4 7.
and 16 5. a
73 25. Ph
1 20.

[n] Gal. 5. 1
17 24 Ro
8 1 2 an
20. 21.

increase more and more in the things which pertain to the kingdom of God, and be changed for the better; they without doubt are regenerate. 6. Whoever are *inclined* to every good work, are most certainly regenerated; for we are in Christ Jesus, by regeneration, *created unto good works.* On the other hand, the following characters have just reason to doubt of their regeneration, (1) As many as *live* not after the *spirit,* but after the *flesh*; for whatsoever *is born of the flesh, is flesh,* who are under the *dominion* of sin, led captive by the snares of satan (2) All they, who *despise* and account as of no value the *means* of grace and salvation. (3) Whoever *rest* in a civilly *honest* and pharisaical life. (4) Whoever stop in the external *professions* of piety, and labour not for the *internal* exercises of it. (5) As many, as were never *deeply* concerned about their salvation, or the spiritual state of their souls.

XXXVIII. *Sixthly.* This subject inculcates upon us, to strive earnestly for the regeneration of others: which is especially incumbent on the *ministers* of God's word. For since the unregenerate can do nothing towards regenerating *themselves,* 'tis necessary, every one should strive therefor; they especially whose business God hath made it *ex officio* (from their office.) And for their encouragement herein, it may be well seriously to consider, (1) That they are *called* hereto by God (2) That, herein they act as *fellow labourers,* with God (3) That, on this account, they are called *fathers,* because they beget spiritual children. (4) How important a thing the human *soul* is. (5) How glorious it is to *win* souls to Christ. So that Austin not improperly declared, that the conversion of a soul exceeded any *miracle.* (6) How *glorious* it will be for them hereafter, in the last day, to have begotten many to a spiritual life. (7) On the other hand, how *disgraceful,* how horrible it will be, to be found guilty of the neglect of *souls.* But in what manner shall they

— labour

Marginal references:

1 Pet. 2 2
Math 18 3
Eph 2. 10
Col. 10 Acts
9 6 Rom 1
9 & 7. 22
2 Pet 1 4 5 6.
7. 8.
Just reasons
reasons for
doubting of
one's regene-
ration.
1 Th 5 6
2 Tim 25 26
Ezr 21 25
13, 26 12 &7
4 5 6 5 6 7 8
4) 2 Tim 2.
25 26 Mat 5
22 Lu 13 11
2 Pet 3 4 5 6
Rom 2 17
6 This sub-
ject inculcates
upon us to
strive earnest-
ly for the re-
generation of
others
Motives
thereto.
2 Tim 3 5
Mat 21 22
5 Jh 53 2
.. 33 51
2 1Cor 13 3
Jer 31 19
Acts 2 5
Acts 20 17
2 Cor 5 18
9. 2 Tim 2
5 20 27
1Cor 3 9
Cor 6 1
1Cor 4 15
Mat 16 25.

labour for the regeneration of others? Anf. 1. By teaching and inftructing them concerning the nature of regeneration as Chrift did Nicodemus.[f] 2. By inculcating the abfolute *neceffity* of regeneration, without which they can neither *fee*, nor *enter* into the kingdom of God.[g] 3. By laying open the unfpeakable *mifery* of thofe who die without regeneration,[h] as in § xxxv. 4. By powerfully reprefenting the happy *condition* of thofe who are truly regenerate, as in § xxxiv. 5. By pointing out the *means*, (*adminicula*) whereby we may become partakers of regenerating grace; fuch as, v. g. (1) To avoid with Nicodemus[i] intimacy with the unregenerate,[k] and feek, as he did, the company and inftruction of thofe, who can point out to us the life of regeneration.[a] (2) To conceive the *feed* of regeneration,[l] the word of God. (3) To urge the promife of the covenant of grace.[m] (4) To groan out with David, *Create within me a clean heart, O God, and renew a right fpirit within me, &c.*[n] 6. By removing *prejudices*, pretences and impediments, by which the unregenerate are wont to block up their way to regeneration; fuch as v. g. (1) That they fhall thereby be obliged to condemn themfelves, and openly expofe all their paft life with the greateft difgrace to themfelves. To which this anfwer may be given, [1] Whatever fmall difgrace it may be, we muft chearfully fubmit to it, if we would avoid eternal difgrace.[o] [2] The very beft of men never were afhamed to confefs their fins and condemn their wicked lives:[p] and by the confent of all chriftians, this is abfolutely neceffary to falvation.[q] [3] 'Tis even an honor to a man, ingenuoufly to retract whatever he hath done amifs,[r] and recount his paft crimes to the glory of divine grace.[s] Obj. 2. That in this way, they muft begin every thing anew, and pull down all that they have been building up before. Anf. What hath been badly built, fhould be pulled down, left it fall of itfelf; as is plainly the cafe

with

[f] John 3. 4 5.
[g] John 3 3.5.
[h] Rom 7. 24.
[i] Tim 2.26.
Luke 13. 3

[i] John 3 2.
[k] Acts 2.38.40

[a] 1 Cor. 4 15
Prov. 13. 20
Eph. 4. 29
[l] 1 Pet. 1.23
[m] 1 Cor. 4. 15
[m] Ezek 36 25
26 27. an
11. 19. Je
32. 39.
[n] Pf. 51. 12.

[o] Dan. 12

[p] Pf. 51.—
[q] 1 Cor 11.
Prov. 28. 1
[r] 2 Cor. 3.
[s] 1 Tim. 1
Tit. 3. 3.
1 Cor. 6. 10

with buildings, whose foundations are rotten and poor.' Obj. 3. That by bringing into doubt all their former conduct, they shall be brought into a state of despair. Ans. (1) It is better to despair here, where there is *hope*, than hereafter to be in *hopeless* despair forever. (2) This salutary despair of their past wrong ways, is really a substantial *hope*, yea, an undoubted means of bringing them back into the way of eternal salvation. Obj. 4. That they can't come up to that *strictness of life*, which belongs to regeneration and the new creature. Ans. (1) 'Tis thro' *straits* and difficulties that we arrive to any thing glorious. " (2) The way is not difficult, but pleasant, to the truly regenerate." Obj. 5. That hereby they shall become exposed, to the censures, reproach and persecutions of the world. Ans. [1] This is the common lot of Christians: and happy is he, in the opinion of Christ, who is *not offended* hereby. ˣ [2] In these very *afflictions* consisteth one of the christian *beatitudes*. ˣ 7. We should seek the regeneration of sinners, by praying for them, that God would give *success* to his own institutions, that he would quicken, illuminate, and renew the unregenerate, and deliver, from their hearts of stone, those who need regeneration, &c.ᶜ Nor need any suspect that in all this, they talk only to the deaf, or knock at the doors of the dead; since, (1) By doing what belongs to them, leaving the success to God, they perform their *bounden* duty and will deliver their own souls. ᵈ (2) Altho' it may so happen that they are treating with those, who are *spiritually* dead; yet they are treating with those who are *naturally* alive, who are endowed with understanding and will, and can understand things in their grammatical and historical sense. (3) Because God, in the use of such means, is wont to bestow the grace of regeneration.

XXXIX.

(marginal references:)
ᵗ Mat 7. 26.

ᵘ Mat. 7 13 14

ʷ Mat 11 28 29 Rom 7 22.

ˣ Mat. 11 6 1 Pet 4. 12 1 Thes 3 3 Mat 5 10 11 1 Pet 4 14 1 Cor 3 5 6 7.

Eph 1 16 17 18 Rom. 5. 13.

Ezek 3. 17 21.

Is. 59. 21. Rom. 15 18 19 1 Cor. 3 5 6 7.

XXXIX. *Seventhly.* This subject may serve to exhort the *regenerate,* diligently to apply to the duties meet for regeneration, viz. (1.) That they acknowledge the unspeakable *grace* of God, bestowed on them in regeneration, by his mere *good pleasure,* while so many thousands are passed by; and that they rejoice therein.[a] (2.) That sensible of this unspeakable benefit, they are abundant in ingenuous *thanksgiving* to God.[b] (3.) That they wholly *depend* on God, as the original fountain of their spiritual life;[c] who worketh in us, both to will, and to do.[d] (4.) That in the use of appointed means, they strive for a continual *increase* of the spiritual life, communicated to them by regeneration.[e] (5.) For this end, they should be importunate with God, in fervent prayer.[f] (6.) Especially should they endeavour with all engagedness to bring forth into the *second* acts (or exercises) the *first act* of spiritual life which they received by regeneration; as they, who *live* by the spirit, should also *walk* in the spirit;[g] and therefore, (7.) Being drawn, they should *run;*[h] being delivered from the heart of stone, they should *make* to themselves *a new heart, and a new spirit;*[i] being circumcised, *they should circumcise themselves to the Lord, and take away more and more the foreskin of their heart.*[k] h. e. Being now made alive by regeneration, they should put off, by *conversion* and repentance, concerning their *former conversation, the old man, and be renewed in the spirit of their mind; and that they might put on the new man which after God is created in righteousness and true holiness.*[l] And that they bear in mind that they are, by regeneration, the *workmanship* of God, *created in Christ Jesus unto good works, that they might walk in them.*[m] But these things, belong to *conversion and sanctification,* which are the end of regeneration, as the *second* acts (or exercises) are the end of the *first* act or principle.

APPENDIX.

---

7 This subject recommends to the regenerate, that they apply diligently to the duties meet for regeneration. What they are.

[a] James 1.17. 18. Eph. 2.5. 6. compared with Luke 15. 32
[b] 1 Pet 1.3.4.
[c] 2 Cor. 4. 4.
5 6.
[d] Phil. 2 13.
[e] 1 Pet. 2. 2.
[f] Ps 51. 12.
[g] Gal. 5. 25. Rom. 8. 1.

[h] Cant. 1. 4.

[i] Ezek 18 31.
[k] Jer. 4. 4.

[l] Eph. 4. 22 23. 24.

[m] Eph. 2. 1

APPENDIX.

FROM the Westminster confession of faith, chap. 10. of effectual calling. "All those whom God hath predestinated unto life, and those only, he is pleased in his appointed and accepted time, effectually to call by his word and Spirit, out of that state of sin and death, in which they are by nature, to grace and salvation by Jesus Christ; enlightening their minds, spiritually and savingly to understand the things of God; taking away their heart of stone, and giving unto them an heart of flesh; renewing their wills, and by his *almighty power determining them* to that which is good; and effectually drawing them to Jesus Christ; yet so as they come most freely, being made willing by his grace.

II. This effectual call is of God's free and special grace alone, not from any thing at all foreseen in man, who is altogether *passive* therein, until being quickened and renewed by the Holy Spirit, he is thereby enabled to answer this call, and to embrace the grace offered and conveyed in it."

Dr. Twiss Prolocutor of the assembly of divines at Westminster in his Vindiciæ Gratiæ, &c. page 15. of the preface, thus defines efficacious grace. "We explain efficacious grace to be an Operation of God affecting the will of man, which is not moral but *physical*, that is immediately and really working in us to do whatsoever good we perform, determining the will to action, but yet so as that it acts freely."

Part III. Page 124. "We do not deny that God acts by (moral) suasion; but he acts also by *a physical* operation, which immediately and immutably affects
the

the will and that by an irrefiftible agency : For as to
moral fuafion, it is plain the agent acts only in the way
of placing objects before the mind, which neither acts
upon the will immediately, nor at all after the manner
of an efficient caufe, but merely after the manner of a
final caufe. This divine concurrence is of that kind
that neither men nor angels can refift. We fay this action of God cannot be refifted, for this reafon, that it
doth not confift in moral fuafion, fo as to be in its nature refiftible ; but in an immediate change of the will,
which cannot properly be called either refiftible or irrefiftible with refpect to the will upon which it acts : For
that, properly fpeaking, is irrefiftible, which a perfon
can not refift tho' he *wills* to. But fuppofing a man fhould
will otherwife, than God worketh in him to will, he not
only *could* refift, but herein actually *would* refift : But
upon this fuppofition it would follow, that God did not
work in him by changing his will ; for if he changed
his will, hereby of unwilling he would make him willing. But if we fuppofe a man to will any thing from
the operation of God, it cannot be that he fhould not
will it or will the contrary. For God himfelf cannot
make a thing to be and not to be at the fame time."

Dr. Ridgley, in his expofition of the larger catechifm
under the anfwer, which treats of effectual calling, Vol.
2. P. 20. gives his fentiments upon the doctrine of regeneration in the following words.

" The firft ftep that he (i. e. God) is pleafed to take
in this work, (i. e. the work of effectual calling) is in
his implanting a principle of fpiritual life and grace,
which is abfolutely neceffary for our attaining to, or receiving advantage by the external call of the gofpel ;
this is generally ftiled regeneration, or the new birth ;
or, as in the fcripture but now referred to, (viz. Ezek.
36. 26.) *a new heart.* If it be enquired, What we are
to underftand by this principle ? We anfwer, That fince
principles are only known by thofe effects they produce,

I   fprings

springs of acting, by the actions themselves, we must be content with this description; that it is something wrought in the heart of man, whereby he is habitually and prevailingly biassed and inclined to what is good: So that by virtue hereof, he freely, readily, and willingly chooses those things which tend to the glory of God; and refuses, abhors and flees from what is contrary thereunto; and, as this more immediately affects the understanding, whereby it is enabled to discern the things which God reveals in the gospel in a spiritual way, it is stiled, his *shining in the heart, to give us the light of the knowledge of his glory, or his giving an eye to see, and an ear to hear.* As it respects the will, it contains in it a power, whereby it is disposed, and enabled to yield the obedience of faith, to what ever God is pleased to reveal to us as a rule of duty, so that we are made willing in the day of his power; and as it respects the affections, they are all disposed to run in a right channel, to desire, delight and rejoice in every thing that is pleasing to God, and flee from ever thing that is provoking to him. This is that whereby a dead sinner is made alive, and so enabled to put forth living actions.

Concerning this principle of grace, let it be observed, that it is infused, and not acquired. The first principle, or spring of good actions, may, with equal reason, be supposed to be infused into us as Christians, as it is undoubtedly true, that the principle of reasoning is infused into us as men: None ever supposed that the natural power of reasoning may be acquired, tho' a greater facility or degree thereof is gradually attained; so that power, whereby we are enabled to put forth supernatural acts of grace, which we call a principle of grace, must be supposed to be implanted in us; which, were it acquired, we could not, properly speaking, be said to be born of God.

From hence I am obliged to infer, that the regenerating act, or implanting this principle of grace, which is,

at

at leaft, in order of nature, antecedent to any act of grace, put forth by us, is the immediate effect of the power of God, which none, who fpeak of regeneration as a divine work, pretend to deny ; and therefore I cannot but conclude, that it is wrought in us *without the inftrumentality of the word, or any of the ordinary means of grace :* My reafon for it is this ; becaufe it is neceffary (from the nature of the thing) to our receiving, improving or reaping any faving advantage by the word, that the fpirit fhould produce the principle of faith ; and to fay, that this is done by the word, is, in effect, to affert that the word produces the principle, and the principle gives efficacy to the word ; which feems to me little lefs than arguing in a circle. The word cannot profit unlefs it be mixed with faith ; and faith cannot be put forth, unlefs it proceeds from a principle of grace implanted ; therefore this principle of grace is not produced by it : We may as well fuppofe, that the prefenting a beautiful picture before a man that is blind, can enable him to fee ; or the violent motion of a withered hand, produce ftrength for action, as we can fuppofe that the prefenting the word, in an objective way, is the inftrument whereby God produces that internal principle, by which we are enabled to embrace it. Neither would this fo well agree with the *idea* of its being a new creature, or our being *created unto good works* ; for then it ought rather to be faid, we are created by faith, which is a good work : This is, in effect, to fay that the principle of grace is produced by the inftrumentality of that which fuppofes its being implanted, and is the refult and confequence thereof.

I am forry that I am obliged in this affertion, to appear, at leaft, to oppofe what has been maintained by many divines of great worth ; who have in all other refpects, explained the doctrine of regeneration, agreeably to the mind and will of God, and the analogy of faith. It may be the principal difference between this
explication,

explication, and their's is, that they speak of regeneration in a large sense, as including in it, not barely the impairing the principle, but the exciting it, and do not sufficiently distinguish between the principle as implanted and deduced into act ; for, I readily own, that the latter is, by the instrumentality of the word, though I cannot think the former so , or, it may be, they consider the principle as excited ; whereas I consider it as created, or wrought in us ; and therefore can no more conclude that the new creation is wrought by an instrument, than I can, that the first creation of all things was.

And I am ready to conjecture, that that which leads many divines into this way of thinking, is the sense in which they understand the words of the apostle : *Being born again, not of corruptible seed, but of incorruptible, by the word of God which liveth and abideth forever :* And elsewhere, *Of his own will, begat he us with the word of truth, that we should be a kind of first-fruits of his creatures.* Whereas this doth not so much respect the implanting the principle of grace, as it does our being enabled to act from that principle ; and 'tis as tho' he should say, he hath made us believers, or induced us to love and obey him by the word of truth, which supposes a principle of grace to have been implanted ; otherwise the word of truth would never have produced these effects. Regeneration may be taken, not only for our being made alive to God, or created unto good works, but for our putting forth living actions, proceeding from that principle which is implanted in the soul. I am far from denying, that faith, and all other graces are wrought in us by the instrumentality of the word ; and it is in this sense that some, who treat on this subject, explain their sentiments, when they speak of being born again by the word · Therefore I persuade myself, that I differ from them only in the acceptation of words, and not in the main substance of the doctrine they maintain."

Doct. Ridgley quotes Charnock, with approbation, concerning

concerning the diſtinction between regeneration and converſion, in the following words. " Regeneration is a
ſpiritual change ; converſion is a ſpiritual motion ; in
regeneration there is a power conferred ; converſion is
the exerciſe of this power ; in regeneration there is given
us a principle to turn ; converſion is our actual turning ;
in the covenant, the new heart, and God's putting the
ſpirit into them, is diſtinguiſhed from their walking in
his ſtatutes, from the firſt ſtep we take in the way of
God, and is ſet down as the cauſe of our motion : In
renewing us God gives us a power ; in converting us
he excites that power. Men are naturally dead, and
have a ſtone upon them ; regeneration is a rolling away
the ſtone from the heart, and a raiſing to newneſs of life ;
and then converſion is as natural to a regenerate man,
as motion is to a living body : A principle of activity
will produce action. The firſt reviving us is wholly
the act of God, without any concurrence of the creature ;
but, after we are revived, we do actively and volunta-
rily, live in his ſight. Regeneration is the motion of
God in the creature ; converſion is the motion of the
creature to God, by virtue of that firſt principle ; from
this principle all the acts of believing, repenting, mor-
tifying, quickening do ſpring. In all theſe a man is active ; in the other he is merely paſſive."*

Thus far Mr. Charnock.

Doct. Ridgley further obſerves, (vol. 2. p. 23) relative to our paſſivity in regeneration. " I cannot but
take notice of a queſtion which frequently occurs under
this head, viz. Whether man in the firſt moment thereof, viz. in regeneration, be merely paſſive, tho' active
in every thing that follows after it ? This we cannot
but affirm, not only againſt the *Pelagians,* but others,
whoſe method of treating the doctrine of divine grace,
ſeems to agree with theirs. This is ſufficiently evident,
not only from the impotency of corrupt nature, as to
what is good, but it's utter averſeneſs thereto, and from
the

the work's being truly and properly divine; or (as has been before obierved) the effect of almighty power. *This is not a controversy of late date*; but has been either defended or oppoied, ever since *Augustine's* and *Pelagius's* time."

With respect to preparatory works, Doct. Ridgly seems well to agree with Van Maftricht. Upon this point he quots Mr. Charnock, in the following words. "Man cannot prepare himself for the new birth: He hath indeed a fubjective capacity for grace, above any other creature in the inferior world; and this is a kind of natural preparation, which other creatures have not; a capacity, in regard of the powers of the foul, tho' not in refpect of the present difpofition of them. He hath an underftanding to know, and when it is enlightened to know God's law; a will to move and run, and when enlarged by grace, to run in the ways of God's commandments; fo that he ftands in an immediate capacity to receive the life of grace, upon the breath and touch of God, which a ftone doth not; for in this it is neceffary, that rational faculties fhould be put as a foundation of fpiritual motions. Tho' the foul be thus capable, as a fubject, to receive the grace of God, yet it is not therefore capable as an agent, to prepare itfelf for it, or produce it. It is capable to receive the truths of God; but as the heart is ftony, it {is incapable to receive the impreffions of thofe truths.

Charnock on regeneration. Vol. 2. p. 147, 148.

Mr. Willard, one of the moft noted New-England divines, in his Expofition upon the leffer catechifm, under the anfwer which refpects effectual calling, p. 433, 434, thus obferves,

" 1. There is fomething habitually wrought in the man, whereby he is capacitated and difpofed to believe in Chrift. And this is ufually called *paffive converfion*. 2. There is fomething done *actually*, by the man in the exciting of this power fo created in him, in which he

· applies

applies thofe graces or powers in him, to their objects, and exercifeth them ; and particularly his faith, in clofing with, and embracing of Jefus Chrift exhibited in the promife ; and is in the gofpel called believing.—Again, he fays, The *act* of faith doth neceffarily fuppofe the *habit* of it, or the power of believing. All acts require a power fuitable and fufficient for them ; nor can any agent go beyond its ability : No effect can exceed the vertue of its caufe : fo that a man muft have faith, in order to his exerting it.

Again. There is no *co operation* of the man with the fpirit in the producing of the habit of faith in him. He is a fubject but not an agent. He contributes nothing at all to it, but it is wholly put into him by another hand. It is a *creating work*, and that belongs to God alone. Eph. 2. 10. It is a refurrection, and that belongs entirely to the divine Omnipotency. Eph. 1. 19. It is a *regeneration*, and none ever helped to beget himfelf, yea, being a *fpiritual regeneration*, none but the fpirit can effect it.

The means themfelves have no efficacy in the production of this habit by moral fuafion. Not but that the fpirit ufeth the means in order to his bringing about this work in us. Ezekiel was to prophefy in order to the dry bones living. Ezek. 37. 9, 10. The means are properly accommodated to work on man as a moral agent, rationally, by evidence or demonftration, by convictions, awakenings, incouragements, and the fpirit comes with them as he fees meet, and gives them fuch an operation : But either their operation is common, and that can at moft be but reparatory ; or it is faving, and then it fuppofeth this habit in them. Moral fuafion can do only on a fubject capable. Come to the grave of a dead man, and make ever fo grave an oration to him, tell him what a miferable condition a ftate of death is, and what benefits accompany the living, and fo beg of him to rife and live ; and what will this do ? There muft be faith, to receive Chrift, e'er the endeavours to perfuade men produce the act of believing on him, *and this is an operation more than merely ethical or moral.*"

Page 435. "All the orthodox consent, that there must be a *new power* put into the man in order to his believing in Christ. That a man can no more of himself come up to the terms of the new covenant, than keep the law of the first covenant. They that deny this are unacquainted with the efficacy of the apostacy, or energy of *original sin* in man. Philosophy tells us that live actions require life in the agent. And spiritual actions must derive from a spiritual life; gracious actions must flow from grace. Call this an habit or a virtue, or a principle; it must be an ability to do these things, which it had not naturally, but must be given it.

This power or ability can be produced by no other, but the Spirit of God. And that because it requires Omnipotency, to the producing of it; and there is none almighty but he. None but he that could make a world, bring light out of darkness, raise the dead, can do this. ——Indeed the Spirit of God in these works find only Impotency in the subject but no resistence; whereas here he meets with, not only a total debility in the creature to join with him in it, but also a malignant opposition to it; there being nothing which the heart of man is more averse to, than coming to Christ and believing in him."

Page 442. As to the necessity of (a legal) conviction of preparation, he thus observes. "This conviction hath no causal influence unto passive conversion. All the necessity that can be urged on that account, is only that of *concomitancy*. The Spirit of God hath done this in such as were not capable of conviction under and by that means. Judicious divines judge that *Jeremiah* and *John* the *Baptist* were converted before they were born. And it is to be believed that elect infants dying in their infancy, have the new creature formed in them, without which they could not be saved. John 3. 3. *Verily, verily I say unto*

unto thee, except a man be born again, he cannot see the king-dom of God. And poſſibly this work is done for others that live, before we are aware of it, who have given evidence of their ſeriouſneſs from their infancy. However, the man can no more convert himſelf upon theſe convictions, than he could before, nor is it eaſier for the ſpirit to do it now. Whenever it is done, it muſt be a creating power, in which God uſeth *no inſtrument, but acts immediately.*"

Page 455. There muſt be a *renewing change* wrought in the *will*, in order to its being enabled to cloſe with Chriſt. Could we ſuppoſe never ſo much light let into the underſtanding, cauſing it to diſcern all the preciouſneſs of Chriſt as he is revealed in the goſpel ; yet if the will remain in the ſame poſture it is, in the man's natural eſtate, it would be impoſſible for it to chuſe Chriſt, and to love him. There muſt therefore be a renovation on it. When therefore the apoſtle had ſpoken of our being *renewed in the image of our mind,* Eph. 4. 23. he exemplifies it with reſpect to the will, verſ. 24. *And that ye put on the new man, which after God is created in righteouſneſs, and true holineſs.* A new underſtanding, without a new heart, will never amount to a thorough converſion. As long as the will remains poſſeſſed of corrupt luſts, and hath no power in it, it can never embrace Chriſt.

This renewing change is wrought, by *creating* a new principle of ſaving grace in the *will* and *affections*. It is certain that if ever the man believe, he muſt have power to believe. This power is that which we call the habit of faith ; which habit is not infuſed by itſelf, but together with all the other regenerating graces, which are wrought in the ſoul by the Spirit. This is that which is called the giving of a new heart, and the putting in of a new ſpirit, &c. Ezek. 36. 26. Which cannot intend new faculties, but a new ſaving impreſſion of grace on the faculties of the ſoul in the man.

K Mr,

Mr. Flavel afferts the *priority* of the work of regene ration to faith in Chrift, in the following words.

" For look as the blood of Chrift is the fountain of all merit, fo the Spirit of Chrift is the fountain of all fpi ritual life. And until he quicken us, (i. e.) infufe the principle of divine life into our fouls, we can put forth no hand, or vital act of faith, to lay hold upon Jefu Chrift.—This his quickening work, is therefore the fir in order of nature to our union with Chrift, and *funda mental* to all other acts of grace done and performed b us, from our firft clofing with Chrift, throughout th whole courfe of our obedience." *Method of grace, fer.* ζ

Mr. Flavel's firft head in the fame difcourfe is, "Briefl to reprefent the neceffary *antecedency* of this quickenin work of the Spirit, to our *firft* clofing with Chrift b faith. This, (he fays) will eafily let itfelf into your un derftanding, if you will but confider the nature of th vital act of faith ; which is the foul's receiving of Chrift and refting upon him for pardon and falvation."

After having infifted upon this *antecedency* of regene ration to faith, he ftarts this *queftion*, and gives the fol lowing *folution.*

" *Queft.* But here it may be doubted, and objecte againft this pofition. If we cannot believe till we a quickened with fpiritual life, as you fay, and cannot b juftified till we believe, as all fay, then it will follow, th a regenerate foul may be in ftate of condemnation for time and confequently perifh, if death fhould befall hi in that juncture."

" *Sol.* To this I return ; That when we fpeak of th *priority* of this quickening work of the Spirit to our actu believing, we rather underftand it of the priority of *na ture,* than of *time,* the nature and order of the work r quiring it to be fo ; a vital principle muft, in order nature be infufed, *before* a vital act can be exerted. Fil make the tree good, and then the fruit good : And ad mit we fhould grant fome priority in *time* alfo to th

quickenin

quickening principle, before actual faith; yet the absurdity mentioned would be no way consequent upon this concession: For as the vital act of faith quickly follows the regenerating principle, so the soul is abundantly secured against the danger objected; God never beginning any special work of grace upon the soul, and then leaving it, and the soul with it, in hazard; but preserves both to the finishing and compleating of his gracious design, Phil. i. 6." *Ibid.*

The same author abundantly asserts, that regeneration is a *supernatural* effect, produced by the exertion of *almighty power*, and that we are therein *wholly passive*. His very doctrine in the above mentioned discourse is this; " That those souls, which have union with Christ, are quickened with a *supernatural* principle of life by the Spirit of God *in order thereunto*."

Again, " As it is said of the two witnesses, Rev. xi. 11. Who lay dead in a civil sense, three days and an half, that the spirit of life from God entered into them; so it is here in a spiritual sense, the spirit of life from God enters into the dead, carnal heart: it is all by way of *supernatural infusion*."——*Ibid.*

Again. "In the next place, according to the method proposed, I am obliged to shew you, that this quickening work is *wholly supernatural*; it is the *sole* and *proper* work of the spirit of God. So Christ himself expresly asserts it, in Joh. 3. 6, 8. *That which is born of the flesh is flesh, and that which is born of the spirit, is spirit:* the wind bloweth where it listeth, and thou hearest the sound thereof, but canst not tell whence it cometh, nor whither it goeth, so is every one that is born of the spirit. Believers are the birth, or offspring of the spirit, who produceth the new creature in them in an unintelligible manner even to themselves. So far is it *above their own ability to produce*, that it is above their capacity to understand the way of its production.——We can *contribute nothing*, I mean *actively*, to the production of this
principle

principle of life. We may indeed be faid to concur *paffively*, with the fpirit in it; that is, there is found in us a capacity, aptnefs or *receptivenefs* of this principle of life. Our nature is endowed with fuch faculties and powers as are meet fubjects to receive, and inftruments to act this fpiritual life: God only quickens the rational nature with fpiritual life."

" It is true alfo, that in the *progrefs* of fanctification, a man doth actively concur with the fpirit; but in the *production* of this principle he *can do nothing*; he can indeed perform thofe external duties that have a remote tendency to it, but he cannot by the power of nature perform any faving act, or contribute any thing more than a *paffive* capacity to the implantation of a new principle: as will appear by the following arguments."

" Arg. 1. He that *actively* concurs to his own regeneration, makes himfelf to differ; but this is denied to all regenerate men, 1 Cor. iv. 7. *Who maketh thee to differ from another? And what haft thou, that thou didft not receive?*"

" Arg. 2. That to which the fcripture afcribes both impotency and enmity with refpect to grace, cannot *actively*, and of itfelf concur to the production of it: but the fcripture afcribes both impotency and enmity to nature, with refpect to grace. It denies to it a power to *do any thing* of itfelf, John xv. 5. And which is lefs, it denies to it a power to fpeak a good *word*, Mat. xii. 34. And which is leaft of all, it denies it power to *think* a good thought. 2 Cor. iii. 5. This impotency, if there were no more, cuts off all pretence of our *active* concurrence. But then, if we confider that it afcribes enmity to our natures, as well as impotency, how clear is the cafe! See Rom. viii. 7. *The carnal mind is* ENMITY *againft God.* And Col. i. 21. *And you that were* ENEMIES *in your minds by wicked works.* So then nature is fo far productive of this principle, as impotency and enmity can enable it to be fo."

" Arg

" Arg. 3. That which is of natural production muſt needs be ſubject to natural diſſolution. That which is born of the fleſh, is fleſh ; a periſhing thing ; for every thing is as its principle is, and there can be no more in the effect than there is in the cauſe. But this princi-ple of ſpiritual life is not ſubject to diſſolution. It is the water which ſprings up into everlaſting life, John. iv. 14. The ſeed of God which remaineth in the rege-nerate, 1 John iii. 9. And all becauſe it is born not of corruptible, but incorruptible ſeed, 1 Pet. 1. 23."

" Arg. 4. If our new birth be our reſurrection, a new creation, yea a victory of our nature, then we cannot *actively* contribute to its production. But under all theſe notions it is repreſented to us in the ſcriptures. It is our reſurrection from the dead, Eph. v. 14. And you know the body is *wholly paſſive* in its reſurrection. But tho' it concurs not, yet it gives pre-exiſtent matter. Therefore the metaphor is deſignedly varied, Eph. iv. 24. Where it is called a *creation* ; in which there is nei-ther active concurrence nor pre-exiſtent matter. But tho' creation excludes pre-exiſtent matter, yet in producing ſomething out of nothing, there is no reluctancy or op-poſition. Therefore to ſhow how purely *ſupernatural* this principle of life is, it is cloathed and repreſented to us in the notion of a *victory*, 2 Cor. x 23. And ſo leaves all to grace."

" Arg. 5. If nature could *produce*, or *actively concur* to the production of this *ſupernatural* life, then the beſt na-tures would be ſooneſt quickened with it ; and the worſt natures not at all, or at laſt, and leaſt of all. But con-trarily, we find the worſt natures often regenerated, and the beſt left in the ſtate of ſpiritual death. With how many ſweet *homiletical* virtues was the young man a-dorned ? Mark x. 21. yet graceleſs ; and what a ſink of ſin was *Mary Magdalen*, Luke vii. 37. Yet ſanctified. Thus beautiful Rachel is barren, while Leah bears chil-dren. And there is ſcarce any thing that affects and

melts

melts the hearts of Chriftians more, than this compara-
tive confideration doth, when they confider veffels of
gold caft away, and leaden ones chofen for fuch noble
ufes.   So that it is plain enough to all wife and hum-
ble fouls, that this new life is *wholly of fupernatural production.*"—*Ibid.*

Again. "But though we cannot pry into thefe fecrets
by the eye of reafon, yet God hath revealed this to us
in his word, that it is wrought by *his own almighty
power*, Eph. i. 19. The apoftle afcribes this work to the
exceeding greatnefs of the power of God.   And this muft
needs be, if we confider, how the fpirit of God expreffes
it in fcripture by a new creation ; (1. e.) a giving being
to fomething, out of nothing, Eph. 2. 10. In this it differs from all the effects of human power ; for men always work upon fome pre-exiftent matter, but here
there is no fuch matter.   All that is in man, the fubject
of this work, is only a *paffive* capacity, or *receptivity*, but
nothing is found in him to *contribute* towards this work.
This *fupernatural* life is not, nor can be educed out of
natural princinles.   This *wholly tranfcends the fphere of
all natural power.*"—*Ibid.*

The teftimony of this author is alfo very exprefs,
that regeneration is effected *inftantaneoufly.*   His words
are thefe, " This infufion of fpiritual life is done *inftantaneoufly*, as all *creation*-work is.   Hence it is refembled
to that *plaftic power*, which in a moment made the light
to fhine out of darknefs ; juft fo God fhines into our
hearts, 2 Cor. iv. 6."

" It is true, a foul may be a long time under the
preparatory work of the fpirit ; he may be under convictions and humiliations, purpofes and refolutions a
long time,—attending the means and ordinances ; but
when the fpirit comes to quicken the foul, it is done
in a moment : even as it is in the infufion of the rational
foul, the body is long e're it is prepared and moulded,
but when once prepared and ready, it is quickened with
the fpirit of life in an INSTANT." *Ibid.*   Doct.

Doct. Wits or Witfius, a noted Dutch divine of the laft age, fometime colleague with *Van Maftricht* in the Profefforfhip at Utrecht, afterwards Regent of the Divinity College of the Sates of Holland and Weft-Friefland, in his *Œconomy of the Covenants* under the head of Effectual Calling, Page 471 of Dr. Crookfhank's tranflation, thus obferves,

" The *external* call will bring none to communion with Chrift, unlefs it be accompanied with the *internal,* which is accomplifhed not only by perfuafion and command, but by the powerful operation of the Spirit. There is a certain call of God, whereby he makes the things, he calls, to exift, by that very call. By fuch a call, *he calleth thofe things which be not, as though they were.* Rom. 4. 17. For, when he faid, let there be light, immediately there was light, Gen. 1. 3. Not unlike this is that internal call of the fpirit, of which the apoftle writes, 2 Cor. 4. 6. *God who commanded the light to fhine out of darknefs, hath fhined in our hearts.*

Here God exerts his infinite power, by which he converts the foul no lefs powerfully than fweetly. He writes his law on their heart, Jer. 31. 33. Puts the reverence of himfelf there, Ezek. 11. 20. And not only calls them from darknefs to his marvellous light ; but alfo, by the call, *draws* them, not to ftand ftill in the path of doubtful deliberation, but to *run after him,* Cant. 1. 4. Not only puts them in an equal poife, but turns them. Jer. 31. 18. Not only advifes, but perfuades, and *he is ftronger and prevails,* Jer. 20. 7. Nor does he follicit, but *tranflate,* Col. 1. 13. Not by an ordinary, but by that mighty power, by which he raifed Chrift from the dead. Eph. 1. 20."

Under the head of regeneration, p. 476. he gives this definition of it, " REGENERATION *is that fupernatural act of God, whereby a new and divine life is infufed into the elect perfon, fpiritually dead, and that from the incorruptible feed of the word of God, made fruitful by the infinite power of the Spirit.*

Spirit. * He then obferves upon the fpiritual death of finners, " that they are fpiritually infenfible of all fpiritual things, and deftitute of all true feeling ;—nor have they any relifh for divine grace, becaufe it has not yet been conferred upon them ; nor any longing after heavenly things, being ignorant of their worth.   They are wholly incapable of every act of true life.—The underftanding is overfpread with difmal darknefs.   The will has no tendency to things unknown : and thus all the things of God are defpifed by it as mean." Page 478.
" By regeneration a new life is put into the elect, refulting from a gracious union with God and his Spirit. For, what the foul is to the body, that God is to the foul.   Moreover, this fpiritual life may be confidered, either by way of *faculty*, and in the *firft act*, in the ufual language of the fchools ; or by way of *operation*, and in the *fecond act*.   In the former refpect, it is that *inward conftitution* of the foul, whereby it is fitted to exert thofe actions, which are acceptable to God in Chrift, by the power of the fpirit uniting it to God : whether fuch actions immediately flow from that principle, or whether they lie concealed for fome time, as fruits in their feed. In the latter refpect, it is that activity of the living foul, by which it acts agreeably to the command of God, and the example of Chrift.

If we confider this firft principle of life, there is not the leaft doubt, but regeneration is accomplifhed in a moment.   For there is no delay in the tranfition from death to life.   No intermediate ftate between the regenerate and unregenerate can be imagined fo much as in thought, if we mean regeneration in the firft act : for

one

* Doct *Witfius* probably intends the fame kind of inftrumentality of the word as Doct. *Van Maftricht*, when he calls it "*only a moral inftrument* of regeneration," and that not fo properly to regeneration in the firft act, (which feems to confift, according to thefe authors, in fructifying or making fruitful the word, or rather in laying a foundation for the words becoming fruitful, in which the word cannot be an inftrument) as to regeneration in the fecond act or confequent exercifes; fee extracts from Doct. Ridgley.

one is either dead or alive : either the child of God, or of the devil ; either in the way to falvation or damnation. There neither is, nor can be any medium here.

Hence it appears, there are no preparations antecedent to the firft beginning of regeneration ; becaufe previous to that, nothing but mere death in the higheft degree is to be found in the perfon to be regenerated. *When we were DEAD IN SINS*, he hath quickened us together with Chrift, Eph. 2. 5. And indeed the fcripture reprefents man's converfion by fuch fimilitudes, as fhow, that all preparations are entirely excluded ; fometimes calling it a *new regeneration* to which, certainly, none can contribute any thing of himfelf : But yet, as natural generation prefuppofes fome difpofitions in the matter ; fo, that we may not imagine any fuch thing to be in ourfelves but from God, we have this held forth by the fimilitude of a *refurrection* ; in which a body is reftored from matter, prepared by no qualifications : yet becaufe here, certainly is matter, but in the refurrection of the foul there is nothing at all, therefore we have added the figure of a *creation*, Pf. 51. 10. Eph. 2. 10. By which we are taught, that a new creature exifts from a fpiritual nothing, which is fin ; but as there was not fomething in nothing, to affift and fuftain creation ; fo there was nothing to oppofe and refift ; but fin is fo far from fubmitting to what God does, that it is reluctant thereto, and in an hoftile manner at enmity with him : accordingly the other images did not fully complete the idea of this admirable action, till at length it is called the *victory* of God : Victory, I fay, over the devil who maintains his palace, Luke 11. 21, and effectually worketh in the children of difobedience, Eph. 2. 2. All thefe operations of God tend to exclude, as much as poffible, all preparations from the beginning of our regeneration."

He then goes on to cenfure the *Semi-pelagians* of Merfeilles, " who infifted that a man comes to the grace whereby we are regenerated in Chrift, by a natural fa-

culty,

culty; as by asking, seeking, knocking, and that, in some at least, before they are born again, there is a kind of repentance going before, together with a sorrow for sin, and a change of life for the better, and a beginning of faith, and an initial love of God, and a desire of grace. And tho' they did not look on these endeavours to be of such importance, as that it could be said, we were thereby rendered worthy of the grace of the Holy Spirit; as *Pelagius* and *Julian* professed? Yet they imagined, they were an *occasion* by which God was moved, to bestow his grace." And likewise the *remonstrants*, who write, that " *some work of man goes before his vivification; namely to acknowledge and bewail his death, to will, and desire deliverance from it; to hunger, thirst and seek after life.*" He observes " there is little accuracy in the reasonings of these men. For, 1st. Since our nature is become like an evil tree, it can produce no fruit truly good and acceptable to God, and do nothing, by which it can prepare itself for the grace of regeneration. 2dly. It has been found, that they, who, in appearance were, in the best manner disposed for regeneration, were yet at the greatest distance from it, as the instance of that young man, Mark 19. 21, 22, very plainly shews. 3dly. And on the other hand, they, who had not even the least appearance of any preparation, as the publicans and harlots, went into the kingdom of God, before those who were civilly righteous and externally religious. 4thly. God testifies, that in the first approach of his grace, *he is found of them, that sought him not, and asked not for him.* Isa. 65. 1. Fulgentius says extremely well: *We have not certainly received grace, because we are willing, but grace is given us, while we are still unwilling.*"

He then observes, p. 483, upon the preparations which have been admitted by some of the reformed as Perkins, Ames, and the British Divines at the Synod of *Dort*, " who have assigned in persons to be regenerated, 1st. A breaking off the natural obstinacy, and a flexibi-

lity

lity of the will. 2. A serious consideration of the law.
3. A consideration of their own fins and offences against
God. 4. A legal fear of punishment, and a dread of
hell, and consequently a despairing of their salvation,
with respect to any thing in themselves." These, he
acknowledges, differ from the favourers of *Pelagianism*
in the following manner, 1st. That they are not for having these things to proceed from nature, but profess
them to be the effects of the spirit of bondage, prepar-
ing a way to himself, for their actual regeneration. 2dly.
That they are not for God's bestowing the grace of regeneration from a regard to, and moved by occasion of,
these preparations, much less by any merit in them ;
but they imagine that God, in this manner, levels a way
for himself, fills up vallies, depresses mountains and hills,
in order the better to smooth the way for his entrance
into that soul." Upon which he observes, "We really
think they argue more accurately, who make these and
the like things in the elect, to be preparations to the
further and more perfect operations of a more noble and
plentiful spirit, and so not preparations for regeneration,
but the fruits and effects of the first regeneration : For
as these things suppose some life of the soul, which spiritually attends to spiritual things, and are operations of
the spirit of God ; when going about to sanctify the
elect ; we cannot but refer them to the spirit of grace
and regeneration."

P. 485. If this matter be more closely considered, we
shall find, that the orthodox differ more in words, and
in the manner of explaining, than in sense and reality.
For, the term, regeneration, is of ambiguous significati-
on ; sometimes it is blended with sanctification, and by
regeneration is understood that action of God, whereby
man, who is now become the friend of God, and endowed with spiritual life, acts in a righteous and holy manner, from infused habits. And then it is certain, there
are some effects of the spirit, by which he usually pre-

pares them for the actings of complete faith and holiness; for, a knowledge of divine truths, a sense of misery, sorrow for sin, hope of pardon, &c. go before any one can fiducially lay hold on Christ, and apply himself to the practice of true godliness.——But sometimes regeneration denotes the first translation of a man from a state of death, to a state of spiritual life; in which sense we take it. And in that sense none of the orthodox, if he will speak consistently with his own principles, can suppose preparatory works to the grace of regeneration"

P 489 " After a principle of spiritual life is infused into the elect soul by regeneration, divine grace does not always proceed therein, in the same method and order. It is possible that for some time, the spirit of the life of Christ may lie, as it were dormant in some (almost in the same manner, as vegetative life in the seed of a plant, or sensitive life in the seed of an animal, or a poetical genius in one born a poet) so as that no vital operations can yet proceed therefrom, tho' savingly united to Christ, the fountain of true life by the spirit. This is the case with respect to elect and regenerate infants, whose is the kingdom of God, and who therefore are reckoned among believers and saints, tho' unqualified thro' age, actually to believe and practise godliness."

Doct. Le Blanc, a noted divine of the Reformed Church in France in the last century, tho' perhaps not entirely friendly himself to the sentiments which *Van Mastricht* has advanced upon the subject of regeneration and efficacious grace; yet *allows* the general sentiments of the reformed church to be such as are conformable to his, as the following extracts shew. In the *Thesis* concerning the distinction between sufficient and efficacious grace among protestants: After giving the sentiments of the Lutherans and Remonstrants, and observing that the Reformed generally renounce the distinction, he thus further explains their sentiments concerning divine grace.

Page 13. " It is the common opinion of all the Reformed who adhere to the synod of Dort, that the grace of God, to which is to be afcribed the converfion of man and all the good works which follow thereupon, is effectual of *itfelf* ; nor doth its efficacy in any meafure depend upon the co-operation or confent of the will of man ; fince it is the infallible caufe of that confent or co-operation. And this is agreeable to the decrees of the Synod of Dort. For that Synod condemn thofe, who teach *that God, in the work of regeneration, doth not put forth his almighty power, whereby he powerfully and infallibly determineth the will to faith and converfion : but that, fuppofing all the operations of grace, which God ufeth in converfion, man can fo refift God and the Spirit, when defigning and willing to regenerate him, and oft times actually doth fo refift, as utterly to hinder his regeneration ; and that therefore it remains in the power of man, whether to be regenerated or not.* They alfo condemn thofe who teach, *that grace and free will are joint caufes concurring together in the beginning of converfion, and that grace in the order of nature doth not precede the efficiency of the will :* that is, *that God doth not efficacioufly affift the will of man to converfion, before the will of man moveth and determineth itfelf.* And how God effecteth a real converfion in the elect, the fame Synod thus explaineth. *He not only caufeth the gofpel to be externally preached unto them and powerfully illuminateth their minds by the Holy Ghoft, fo as rightly to underftand and difcern the things of the Spirit of God ; but by the efficacy of the fame Spirit, in his regenerating influences, He penetrateth the inmoft receffes of the foul ; openeth their clofed hearts ; fofteneth their hard hearts ; circumcifeth their uncircumcifed hearts ; infufeth new qualites into the will ; and of dead, maketh it alive ; of evil, maketh it good ; of unwilling, maketh it willing ; of difobedient, obedient ; and leadeth and ftrengthneth it ; fo that it is enabled, like a good tree, to bring forth fruit in good actions.* And in the next article they add, this operation of God is entirely fupernatural, alfo moft powerful and pleafant,
wonderful,

wonderfu', fecret, and ineffable ; not lefs than, or inferior to, the power exerted in creation, or the refurrection of the dead ; fo that all they, in whofe hearts God
worketh in this wonderful manner, are certainly, infallibly, and effectually regenerated and converted."

Page 15. " Altho' the divines of the Reformed
Church agree in this, that grace worketh effectually, not
only upon the underftanding, but alfo upon the will of
man, and that the will is powerfully and infallibly turned and determined thereby to that which is good ; yet
there is fome difference among them, about the *manner*
in which grace affecteth the will ; fo that in confequence
thereof it fhould turn to God, and confent to that which
is good."

He then fpeaks of feveral, as *Teftard, Amyrald* and
Cameron, who fuppofe the will always to follow the laft
dictate of the underftanding ; and that the will is changed and renewed by a powerful illumination of the underftanding, agreeably to what is obferved by *Van Maftricht* concerning *Cameron* and others, § xxvi. "But (faith
he) other divines of the Reformed Church hold, that the
immediate operation of grace affecteth, not only the underftanding, by illuminating of it ; and infufing new
light into it, but alfo the will, in which it really and
phyfically worketh that confent which it yields to the divine commands. This opinion Doct. *Ames* lays down
and explains in his *Bellarminus enervatus,* lib. iii° *de gratia cap* 3 *We hold,* faith he, *that together with moral
fuafion there is joined a real efficiency of God, by which a new
principle of fpiritual life is effectually wrought in the heart of
man, and he at the fame time excited to put forth the acts of
that life.* In the fame place he fully approves and acknowledges as his, the fentiment of *Didacus Alvares,*
which is that God by the affiftance of his grace doth
phyfically or after the manner of a phyfical caufe, effectually predetermine the will of the creature, fo that he
infallibly confenteth and co-operateth with God, cal-

ling and inviting him. And afterwards uſing the words of Alvares, he ſaith, that phyſically to pre-determine the will is nothing elſe than truly, efficiently or really to make the will infallibly to co-operate with God."

This ſame author further obſerves, p. 19. "That there is a ſeeming contradiction in the ſentiments of the reformed ; who univerſally hold that man freely puts forth the firſt act of converſion, and yet that he is *merely paſſive* in the work of regeneration and converſion , for how can the will of man freely put forth the act of converſion, and yet at the ſame time be merely paſſive in converſion ? Can the will be merely paſſive, when it is ſuppoſed to operate freely ?"

" The Britiſh divines (he obſerves) in the acts of the ſynod of Dort, ſolve this difficulty, by obſerving that converſion is to be taken in a two-fold ſenſe; 1ſt. As it denoteth the immediate work of God in regeneration : 2dly. As it denoteth the action of the man in turning to God, by ſaving faith and repentance. In the work of regeneration or converſion, taken in the firſt ſenſe, according to them, man is merely paſſive, nor is it in the power of the will of man to hinder God thus immediately converting and regenerating : But in converſion, taken in the other ſenſe, the will being influenced by God, is active, and putteth forth thoſe actions, in which our converſion to God conſiſteth. But converſion, as it denoteth the immediate work of God, they ſay, is that whereby he regenerateth, and as it were createth anew, by an internal and wonderful operation the ſouls of his elect, who have been before exerciſed and prepared by various workings of his grace ; infuſing into them a quickening ſpirit, and endowing all the faculties of the ſoul with new qualities."

Much to the ſame purpoſe ('tis obſerved) was the opinion of the *Heſſian* divines, at the ſame ſynod, which he gives us in the following words, " *The will of man, in the reception of ſupernatural qualities or faculties and power,*

and

*and also in the reception of new inclinations, is merely passive:
So that the action of the Holy Spirit infusing that supernatural
power into the will, & turning & inclining the will effectually &
powerfully to faith & conversion, doth not depend upon the will
of man or any co-operation or consent of it.* But to the acts of
*faith, love, hope,&c. and all good exercises, a man is not merely
passive, but both passive and active, since, being influenced and
moved by the previous grace of God, and assisted by his subse-
quent grace, he is active in the exercises of faith, love, hope and
other virtues.*"

Doct. Ames, professor of divinity in the university of
Franaker, in his work entituled *Medulla Theologiæ* in the
chapter concerning effectual calling, from sect. 20, to
25, thus observes, " The reception of Christ, with respect to man, is either passive or active, Phil. 3. 12.
*That I may apprehend that for which also I am apprehended
of Christ.* The passive reception of Christ is that, by
which a spiritual principle of grace is begotten in the
will of man. Eph. 2. 5. *He hath quickened us.* For this
grace is the foundation of that relation, wherein we are
united to Christ. John 3. 3. *Except a man be born again,
he cannot see the kingdom of God.* The will is the most
proper and primary subject of this grace, because the
conversion of the will is the effectual principle of the
conversion of the whole man, Phil. 2. 13. *For it is God
that worketh in you both to will and to do of his good pleasure.*
An illumination of the mind is not sufficient to produce
this effect, because it doth not take away that corruption
which is seated in the will, nor doth it communicate
thereto, any new supernatural principle, whereby it can
convert itself. The will however, with respect to this
first reception, is not to be considered either as freely
active, nor as irrationally passive ; but as a subject capable of obeying the divine impression, 2 Cor. 4. 6. *For
God who commanded the light to shine out of darkness, hath
shined in our hearts,*" &c.

Mr.

Mr. Rutherford, a noted Scotch divine of the laft century, in his *Exercitationes apologeticæ pro gratiâ divinâ,* gives his fentiments relative to the will's following the laft dictate of the underftanding (which are agreeable to the fentiments of Van Maftricht) in the following words, p. 366.

" If the laft judgment of the underftanding neceffarily and of itfelf determined the will, grace would become mere fuafion, nor would any internal grace be neceffary to cure the will ; to remove the darknefs of the mind and inftruct it in what it is ignorant of would be fufficient, *which is the grace of Pelagians.* And thus the mind of a reprobate perfon, by an acquired habit of faith, and by clear objective evidence, might be fo taught (as appears to me poffible in the prefent cafe) as to difcern in a propofed act of obedience, 1. The facility. 2. The pleafure. 3. The utility ; and that the will fhould not in the prefent cafe (as it might do) turn the mind to confider, either the difficulty of it, or any other thing, wherein it might appear as difagreeable, and that the will fhould not turn the mind, from the contemplation of this act, to earthly confiderations. In this cafe a perfon might believe, without his will's ever being healed, and perform a fupernatural act ; nor would there be any need of taking away the heart of ftone and putting within us a heart of flefh. Nor do thofe places of fcripture, which are commonly objected here, prove the contrary, as Pf. 9. 10. *And they that know thy name will put their truft in thee.* If this knowledge (fay they) did not determine the will, it might be that they that know the name of God would not truft in the LORD. And alfo John 4. 10. *If thou kneweft the gift of God, and who it is that faith unto thee, give me to drink ; thou wouldft have afked of him, and he would have given thee living water.* Now if this knowledge would not determine the will to afk living water of *Chrift,* then the woman might have known the gift of God, and yet not have afked living

.water

water of him ; and so the words of Christ would not have been true. Ans. In such like propositions, there is always understood the physical agency of God, otherwise if it be taken exactly literal, it would follow that a speculative knowledge of the object would be sufficient for the act of faith, without the infusion of a new power ; which no one will pretend."

Doct. *Burman*, professor of divinity in the university of *Utrecht* thus observes, relative to the insufficiency of illumination to renew the will, p. 227, of his *Theologiæ synopsis*, "Sanctification *immediately* effects the will, which the very learned *Cameron* wrongly denied, asserting that the other faculties of the soul were rectified and perfected by the light of the understanding, that the will is not immediately affected ; but always follows the last dictate of the understanding. Which are wrongly connected together ; since the order and connection of these faculties, or the power and dominion which the understanding exerciseth over the will, is not such, that the will implicitly followeth the signal held up by the understanding. Hence it happens that corruption doth, in some sense, cleave more strongly to the will, or more deeply affects it, than it doth the understanding ; hence the will cannot be excited, or move itself, according to the light of the understanding alone. That the illumination of the understanding is not sufficient, we have full proof daily from those who are reprobate. There must be, over and above the illumination of the understanding, an *attention in the will* : Which being supposed the inclination of the will followeth the clear perception of the understanding. But this attention is the gift of God, as appears in the case of Lydia. Acts 16. 14.

Both Rutherford and Burman are full in asserting the *priority* of regeneration to any gracious exercise, our *passivity* therein, its being a *physical* and not a moral operation, its irresistibility, &c.

Doct. Braunius professor of divinity at *Groningen* after confuting

confuting many falfe notions of divine grace held by the Papifts, Remonftrants, &c. fuch as that it confifts in moral fuafion, in an external illumination, &c. he obferves, "That the grace of God ought to be conceived of as a new creation."—"That hereby God difpeleth the darknefs of the mind, enkindleth the light of truth, fofteneth and bendeth the will; yea as it were createth it anew, reproduceth it, and raifeth it from the dead, and powerfully, and fweetly determineth it to good, fo that it moft freely wills and embraces it."— " Therefore the will of man is merely *paffive* in the firft moment of the divine operation; is paffive in being fashioned by God according to his good pleafure."— " Hence the apoftle well obferves, that the will of man with refpect to the grace of God is as clay in the hands of the potter, from whom it wholly receives it's form." Doctrina Fiderum. p. 528. 529, 530.

With refpect to an illumination of the underftanding's being fufficient for fanctification, he thus obferves, " They are wrong, who teach that fanctification confifteth only in the underftanding; fince it confifteth in the underftanding and will together. The underftanding can exercife no dominion over the will, but is merely paffive in the reception of objects, as they offer themfelves: But the will chufeth what it judgeth to be beft. The underftanding therefore ought to be enlightened, that it may rightly receive objects and propofe them to the will. The will muft be renewed, that it may chufe the greateft good. Nor doth it follow, from the will's following the laft practical judgment, that the underftanding only needs to be fanctified, and not the will; fince this laft practical judgment is the work of the will; for the will judgeth; not the underftanding."

'Tis plain our author means by the underftanding the fimple faculty of perception; and when he excludes judgment from the underftanding, he means the practical judgment, or that which refpects our practice, and not things merely fpeculative. In which fenfe perhaps his opinion, which at firft view appears fingular, may be not wide from the truth.

To thefe quotations I will add a few words from Mr.
Brine, a late ingenious writer in England. Page 126,
of his book, entituled, *A treatife upon various fubjects.*

"Regeneration preceeds and may be confidered, as
the foundation and fpring of converfion and fanctification. For that is the principle from which both arife.
Grace as a principle of fpiritual acts, is firft communicated, and from that proceed all acts of a holy fpiritual
nature, both internal and external. Neither of the latter
can be until the firft is wrought. And when that is
effected, both the latter certainly follow. In the firft we
are merely paffive, in converfion and fanctification we
are active.'

P. 101. "Regeneration is the infufion of a new principle of fpiritual life. Naturally men are dead in tref-
paffes and fins, and, therefore, in order to their acting
in a holy and fpiritual manner, a living holy principle
muft be communicated to them. Hence the faints are
faid to be quickened, that is to fay, they are infpired
with life. And this is a new life, and is a fpring of
new actions. It is called a new heart, and a new fpirit,
and a heart of flefh ; grace is not our old nature made
better, and excited unto fpiritual acts ; but it is a new
nature produced in our minds, by the infinite power
and grace of God. For which reafon we are faid to be
new creatures. Something now exifts in us, which had
nothing in our minds before. Nothing fhort of this
comes up to the fcriptural account of this matter. No
excitations, no impulfes, no aids, however forcible and
great they are fuppofed to be, reach the intention of the
holy Spirit in thofe phrafes, which he ufes on this fubject. Befides our corrupt nature is not a fit fubject for
heavenly excitations, nor is it poffible to bring it in fubjection to the obedience of Chrift. The carnal mind
can never become fubject to the law of Chrift. A bitter
fountain will as foon fend forth fweet ftreams, which
all know is impoffible. Regeneration doth not confift

in acts, but in the production of a principle diſpoſed unto actions holy and well pleaſing unto God, by *Jeſus Chriſt* ; and therefore this work is inſtantaneous and wrought on the mind at once."

"By converſion I underſtand, what may be called the *primary* actings of the regenerate principle. Before I proceed in diſcourſing on which, I would premiſe two things. One is, the human mind, as it ſeems to me, is one rational principle of operation. The *ſchools* have taught us, that there are three diſtinct powers of the human ſoul, *viz.* The underſtanding : The will ; and the affections. They have done this for the ſake of accuracy, in ſpeaking of the diſtinct actions of our minds. I much queſtion whether this is according to truth in philoſophy, and I can't but apprehend, that it hath not been ſerviceably to the cauſe of truth in divinity, particularly, in treating on the ſubject now under conſideration.

It ſeems to me, that our intelligent nature is one power, and not the ſubject of different and diſtinct powers, but capable of exerting itſelf, in various modes. In perception, willing, nilling, loving, hating, &c. The other thing I would premiſe is this : That grace is one ſpiritual principle of operation in the ſoul, and not, properly ſpeaking, various and diſtinct habits ſeated in our mind ; but able to exert itſelf after diverſe ways. As, in ſpiritual perception, holy chuſing and refuſing, loving and delighting in ſpiritual things, in a ſpiritual manner, which are commonly ſpoken of as acts of ſo many different and diſtinct habits of Grace in our minds ; but I think, that they all proceed from one principle, as their common root and ſpring. If this is true, thoſe conteſts, which have ariſen and been litigated between learned men, concerning grace as having one power of the mind only for its ſubject, and concerning the impropriety of ſuppoſing, that the grace of faith is ſeated in two powers of the ſoul, *viz.* the underſtanding and the will far, which is true, those contests may soon be issued, and that it is not, I am humbly of opinion, neither philofophy, nor religion will prove."

It should have been observed to the reader, that by the REFORMED, or the *reformed church*, foreign writers mean all denominations of Proteftants, except the Lutherans (with refpect to whom they are called reformed) and fome heretical fects that have fprung up among them, as the *Socinians*, *Arminians*, &c.

This publication would have been rendered more compleat by quotations from Turretine and the doings of the famous Synod of Dort, had not the publifher been difappointed about procuring thefe books.

N. B. The Synod of Dort mentioned by Van Maftricht, Le Blanc, &c. confifted of delegates from the whole Reformed Church, was called by the States of Holland in the reign of King James the Firft, to confider the Arminian herefy, which was condemned by that Synod.

ERRATA.

Page 28. line 19. for *thefe* read *thofe*. P. 44. l. 19. after *confirms*, add *than deftroys*. P. 53. l. 22. for *enabled* read *enobled*. P. 56. l. 6. for *pure* read *purer*. Ibid 'aft line, for *their* read *the*. Before law read *the*. P. 81. l. 12. for *regeneration* read *generation*.

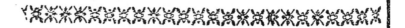

Lightning Source UK Ltd.
Milton Keynes UK
UKHW030756050123
414875UK00008B/491